"Watching & Working"

An Inductive Study of The Book of Nehemiah

I am doing a great work, so that I cannot come down.
Why should the work cease…Nehemiah 6:3

Published By
Morningstar Christian Chapel
Whittier, California 90603

"Watching and Working"
An Inductive Study through the book of Nehemiah

Published by Morningstar Christian Chapel
ISBN: 978-0-9729477-7-0

Additional copies of this book are available by contacting:

Morningstar Christian Chapel
Whittier, California 90603
562.943.0297

Watching and Working

Introduction

As we begin our study of the Book of Nehemiah, we will learn invaluable lessons that will tremendously strengthen and encourage us in our walk with our Lord Jesus Christ.

The Book of Nehemiah is one of the best Old Testament books on the subject of our service to God. During Nehemiah's life, he served as the cupbearer to the king, a builder of walls and a mighty servant leader of God's people.

Nehemiah's life is an example of the Biblical truth, if we are faithful in the little, God will indeed entrust much to us.

Through this study we will be taught how to deal with a difficult boss, how to balance faith with personal planning, when to act and when to simply continue to wait upon God. We will learn how to cope with delays in answered prayer, how to face seemingly impossible circumstances, and how to stand firm while undeserved criticism comes our way as we serve the Lord.

Nehemiah is a book about vision and God's power; a book of hope and encouragement. I pray that through the study of Nehemiah's life you will find yourself wanting to be more like this strong man of faith who obeyed the Lord as he bravely returned to Jerusalem, God's holy city, when few were willing to follow the call.

Nehemiah will show us, that more often than not, God works in quiet uneventful ways, behind the scenes and without much fanfare, unnoticed to all but the spiritual onlooker whose ear is attuned to God's still small voice.

Nehemiah will start on his knees alone before God and receive a vision, and then because he was willing to answer the call a remnant nation would soon share in his vision and begin to

worship and serve God. There are great lessons in leadership in the book of Nehemiah and from them we begin to understand that a leader can raise up a body of servants loving God, or a body of cynics who complain and serve themselves.

The Book of Nehemiah records Nehemiah's return to Jerusalem from exile in Babylon (445 B.C.). This return from exile began with the order given by Cyrus, king of Persia, in 536 B.C. (Ezra 1). Three companies of exiles returned to Jerusalem. Zerubbabel in 539-530 B.C led the first group of about 5000. During this time the foundation of the Temple was laid before the work was stopped by opposition and by the selfish living of the people. The Temple was completed under the leadership of the prophets Haggai and Zechariah, in 516 B.C. The second return was led by Ezra in 457 B.C. and brought another 2000 back to Jerusalem. Under Ezra's leadership the Biblical reforms were made and worship was restored. This brings us to Nehemiah and the third wave of exiles that returned to Jerusalem in 445 B.C., they came 12 years later than Ezra and 91 years after the first group with Zerubbabel. What they found was a city in disrepair, with no walls for protection, and the people of God in Jerusalem still living in desolation, shame and affliction. The Lord sent a man to rectify this problem...Are you ready to take a challenging journey with Nehemiah? Be prepared to be transformed!

Watching and Working - Outline

I. God's Work Begins in your Heart
Nehemiah 1

II. Waiting: A Time to Make Ready
Nehemiah 2:1-10

III. A Vision in the Making
Nehemiah 2:11-20

IV. Expect Opposition
Nehemiah 2:10 & 4:1-12

V. Mind to Work, Heart to Pray, Eye to Watch
Nehemiah 3:1-4:9

VI. Don't Leave the Building for the Battle
Nehemiah 4:10-23

VII. Satan's Next Ploy: Attacks from Within
Nehemiah 5:1-13

VIII. Leading By Example
Nehemiah 5:14-19

IX. Perseverance in Action
Nehemiah 6

X. Steps to Personal Revival
Nehemiah 7-8

XI. A Nation Returns Home
Nehemiah 9

XII. Setting Biblical Goals
Nehemiah 10

XIII. A Place for All and All in Their Places
Nehemiah 11

XIV. Joy on the Wall
Nehemiah 12

XV. Daily Diligence Needed (Part 1)
Nehemiah 13:1-14

XVI. Daily Diligence Needed (Part 2)
Nehemiah 13:15-31

Lesson Index

Remember to always begin every session of Bible Study in prayer.
It is the Holy Spirit that teaches us and reveals the truth of God's Word to us.

However, when He, the Spirit of truth, has come, He will guide you into all truth; for He will not speak on His own authority, but whatever He hears He will speak; and He will tell you things to come. He will glorify Me, for He will take of what is Mine and declare it to you. (John 16:13, 14)

Timeline of Major Events in Israel's History Prior to the Time of Nehemiah

971 BC Solomon begins to reign as King of Israel
931 BC Kingdom Divided – Israel (North) & Judah (South)
722 BC Fall of Israel – To the Assyrians
606 BC First Siege of the Babylonians against Judah
586 BC Fall of Judah – Exile to Babylon
536 BC King Cyrus of Persia issues a decree – To restore and rebuild Jerusalem
Zerubbabel returns to Jerusalem – foundation of the Temple is laid
520 BC Temple building resumes – completed in 516 BC
457 BC Ezra returns to Jerusalem to restore worship and Biblical reforms
445 BC Nehemiah granted permission to return to rebuild the walls of the Holy City

DAY 1 – BEGIN IN PRAYER

1. Read Nehemiah 1.

2. Who is the author of this book?

3. When was it written? Where was he living?

4. What message did he receive? How did the news affect him?

5. What action did he take?

6. What lessons can you learn from this first reading of Nehemiah 1 that you will be able to apply in your walk with the Lord today?

DAY 2 – BEGIN IN PRAYER

1. Read Nehemiah 1:1-4.

2. The name Nehemiah means Jehovah comforts, he was the son of Hachaliah whose name means whom the Lord enlightens. What does this tell you about Nehemiah's family even though they were in captivity in the land of idolatrous Babylon?

3. Verse 1 sets the scene for us - It came to pass in the month of Chislev, in the twentieth year...Chislev is the ninth month of the Jewish calendar, it usually corresponds to November/December on our calendar. It was winter of 446 BC, in the 20th year of the reign of Artaxerxes of Persia and Nehemiah was living in the citadel, the royal palace, in Shushan (Susa in Hebrew). A remnant of Jews had returned to Jerusalem over the last 90 years, what news does Nehemiah receive from his brother who had returned from Judah?

   Nehemiah was born in Babylonian captivity, he had never seen the city of Jerusalem or the Temple, and yet terrible news about the welfare of the people and the city caused him great heartache. To Whom did he go with his broken heart? (v. 4)

   When tragic news comes your way or when you are facing circumstances that are seemingly impossible to understand, to Whom are you to run?

   a. Psalm 91:14-16

   b. Psalm 145:18-20

   c. Isaiah 55:6, 7

   d. Jeremiah 29:11-13

4. The account of Nehemiah's calling by God and his obedience to answer and be used by the Lord will give us great lessons and deep insight into how the Lord desires to use us, His followers, in the days in which we live. The first important lesson from Nehemiah is found here in chapter 1. The lesson is this...

   God's call to ministry and service to Him always begins with an individual heart. Nehemiah's calling began with a heart moved by God. No one had to twist his arm or apply heavy guilt and pressure; God had touched Nehemiah's heart with an over whelming passion for the city of Jerusalem and the people of God. How is this lesson further illustrated in the following Scriptures and in the lives of the men who were compelled by passion to obey the Lord?

   a. Jeremiah 20:7-9

   b. Acts 4:18-21

   c. 1Corinthians 9:16

What does 1Timothy 3:1 teach us about those who desire to serve the Lord in a position of leadership?

5. The Holy Spirit moves individuals by stirring their heart for a particular need, how does 1Corinthians 12:11, 12 address this truth?

According to 1Corinthians 12:14-26, how does this body, which is made up of many members, work most effectively? What causes it to be the least effective?

Personal: What area of service or ministry has the Lord called you to? Are you doing it as a result of a great burning passion, by constraint, or by habit? It is God's desire, through the moving of the Holy Spirit, to use His children to accomplish His mighty work – if your passion is missing or has diminished, will you begin each day asking the Lord to clearly reveal your gift and calling – for His glory?

6. Choose a verse from today's study to be your memory verse for the week. Record it here and begin to memorize it today!

DAY 3 – BEGIN IN PRAYER

1. Read Nehemiah 1:1-4.

2. The report that Nehemiah received from Hanani was very discouraging. Jerusalem was still lying in ruins (for 161 years now). The city was vulnerable, having no walls for protection from the enemy and the people were in great distress and reproach. What does 2Chronicles 6:4-6 tell us about the Holy City of Jerusalem?

3. The place God had chosen to put His name was no longer a place of glory to the Lord or His people but a ground for thieves and rogues. This tragic news broke Nehemiah's heart. The second important lesson from the life and calling of Nehemiah is this: God's call to ministry is most often discovered in what breaks your heart. According to verse 4, what did Nehemiah do when he suffered a broken heart?

Use a Dictionary of Bible Words to define each of the following words from Nehemiah 1:4:

a. Weep

b. Mourn

c. Fast

d. Pray

Personal: What is it that breaks your heart in the world in which you live?

4. What caused the following people of God to weep and mourn?

a. 1Samuel 1:7-10

b. 2Chronicles 34:21-28

c. Esther 4:3 & 8:3

d. Mark 14:72

e. Luke 19:41-44

5. Nehemiah wept alone for Jerusalem – so had Daniel, Habakkuk, and many other prophets. He had heard enough – it was time to seek God for ways to fix it! The best servants of the Lord are those who have felt the pressure themselves first. They see the need; they have a zeal for the work and serve out of love, not obligation. Nehemiah came before the Lord to offer his broken heart and his willing and available life. God would use him to build the walls, but to do so he must first weep over the ruins. What does the Lord look for in those He uses to accomplish HIS work?

    a. Psalm 24:3-5

    b. Psalm 34:18

6. Record your memory verse for this week and spend time committing it to memory today. Remember the importance of hiding God's word in your heart!

DAY 4 – BEGIN IN PRAYER

1. Read Nehemiah 1:5-7.

2. Nehemiah's concern led to mourning, which then led to moving and planning. The third important lesson from the life and calling of Nehemiah is this: Weeping and mourning leads to seeking God with fasting and prayer. Drastic needs drive us first to weep and mourn and then our next stop must

be that of falling on our knees in fasting and prayer. Nehemiah didn't run off with crazy, "I can fix it plans" – he ran to the Lord for direction. What does Isaiah 58:5-10 teach us regarding the correct reason and motivation for fasting?

What instruction did Jesus give us in Matthew 6:16-18 for those times when we are led to fast?

3. After despair came determination! Instead of focusing on what seemed to be insurmountable circumstances, Nehemiah chose to fix his attention upon God. What do you learn from the way Nehemiah began his prayer that will help you in the challenges you face today?

As God's children, we have been given great and precious promises regarding the privilege and responsibility of prayer. What do we learn from these Scriptures that should cause us to be more faithful in prayer?

a. Jeremiah 33:3

b. Psalm 91:14-16

c. Isaiah 55:6, 7

d. Luke 11:9, 10

4. What instruction are we given regarding our personal prayer life?

a. Luke 18:1

b. 1Thessalonians 5:17

c. Colossians 4:2

5. First, Nehemiah focuses his attention on the Almighty, Powerful, True and Living God, which significantly decreases any problem we face! What does Nehemiah declare next in his prayer before the Lord?

Nehemiah admits that the trouble of the nation was self-inflicted for they had sinned against God. He took responsibility along with the nation. Often when trouble comes our way we blame others. How does the confession and repentance in Nehemiah's prayer show us the attitude with which we must come to the Lord in prayer?

What promise is given in 1John 1:9 regarding our confession and repentance?

6. Can you record your memory verse for this week without looking? If not, spend extra time working on it today!

DAY 5 – BEGIN IN PRAYER

1. Read Nehemiah 1:8-11.

2. Nehemiah understood the captivity and suffering of his people were a direct result of the people's sin. While his heart broke over the condition of the holy city, many of the Jews were still comfortably settled in Babylon with no concern for the land of God or the ways of God. Nehemiah desired to receive God's blessings, so what characteristic of God's nature does Nehemiah appeal to for mercy? (vs. 8-9)

What promise had the LORD made to His people should they find themselves separated from His fellowship because of their sin?

3. Read the words of the Lord from Deuteronomy 28:63-64. What was to be the punishment for disobedience?

According to Deuteronomy 28:1-10, what was the LORD'S promise if they had obeyed?

What does Deuteronomy 30:1-10 tell us regarding God's promise to His children when they repented of their sin?

4. In his prayer Nehemiah reminds God of His promises and what He had done for them. There is no better way to pray than to begin by remembering what God has done on our behalf. How do the following Scriptures illustrate the importance of remembering God's faithful promises to you?

   a. Psalm 63:6-8

   b. Psalm 77:10-15

   c. Psalm 111:1-5

   d. Psalm 143:3-6

Personal: If you began every prayer reminding yourself of the awesome, faithful, and mighty power of your Heavenly Father, how might your prayers be changed? If you haven't made it your habit, why don't you start today!

5. The fourth important lesson from the life and calling of Nehemiah is found in verse 11. He had seen a great need, it had broken His heart, He sought the

Lord in fasting and prayer and here we find lesson number four: He made himself available! Some gripe and complain about their needs not being met in their church or community. The one who is sensitive to God's calling and obedient to His Spirit will respond like the prophet Isaiah. According to Isaiah 6:5-8, Who did he see, how did he react, and what was his response?

What was the response of one very young servant of the Lord to God's calling on her life recorded in Luke 1:26-38?

What was Nehemiah's request in verse 11?

What was Nehemiah's job?

Drawing from what you know about the nature of a monarchy, why was it dangerous for Nehemiah to bring his request before the king he served?

What does Proverbs 21:1 say that ought to help you when you choose to make yourself available to the Lord and it seems as though someone is standing in your way or hindering your progress?

6. Can you record your memory verse for this week without looking? If not, spend extra time working on it today!

DAY 6 – BEGIN IN PRAYER

1. Read Nehemiah 1.

2. Make a list of the specific lessons we learned from studying Nehemiah's calling to service:

Lesson #1

Lesson #2

Lesson #3

Lesson #4

3. What is it in your life and world that is breaking your heart? Begin to seek the Lord about what He wants you to do about it.

4. Record your memory verse and reference without looking!

DAY 1 – BEGIN IN PRAYER

1. Read Nehemiah 2:1-10.

2. What happened one day while Nehemiah was faithfully serving the king?

How did Nehemiah respond to the king's question?

Does it appear that he had thought about how to answer to this question if it was asked of him?

What was the king's response?

To Whom did Nehemiah give the credit for this awesome turn of events?

Who wasn't pleased to see Nehemiah come to Jerusalem?

3. What lessons can you learn from this first reading of Nehemiah 2:1-10 that you will be able to apply in your walk with the Lord today?

DAY 2 – BEGIN IN PRAYER

1. Read Nehemiah 2:1-10.

2. From chapter one we learned that God begins a great work by capturing a surrendered heart, and often that which breaks your heart determines the calling of God. We saw Nehemiah, not overwhelmed by the circumstances or difficulties, but rather turning to God in confession of sin, in faith in His Word, and in prayer and fasting to discover God's will. Lastly, Nehemiah made himself available to be the vessel that God would use. But, then he had to wait! Is it hard for you to wait? Why?

3. What are we taught in the following Scriptures about waiting for God's perfect timing?

a. Psalm 25:20, 21

b. Psalm 27:14

c. Psalm 33:20-22

d. Psalm 62:1, 5-7

4. It certainly had been a time of waiting for Nehemiah! Over 4 months had passed and the burning desire in his heart to answer God's call still filled his thoughts and his prayers, but he was unable to act. We all have to deal with authorities in our lives that influence or rule over us. It might be a parent, a teacher, or an employer; it might be a policeman, a mayor, or a governor. As believers, we are called to submit our lives to those who have been given responsibility to rule. What instructions are we given regarding this submission?

    a. Romans 13:1, 2

    b. Titus 3:1

    c. 1Peter 2:13-17

How do these truths apply if the one who has authority over you is an unbeliever living in sin, who makes poor, selfish, or even evil choices?

How would you characterize the king under whom Nehemiah served?

5. So, why does God have us wait? Perhaps at times it is simply to weed out the uncalled or the emotional responder whose heart for the project lasts until the next need is presented. Sometimes delays will help in purifying our desires and strengthening our confidence and dependency upon God. How do the following examples encourage you in your waiting?

   a. 1Samuel 1:1-20

   b. Daniel 10:1-15

What does Luke 18:1-8 add to your understanding of the importance and the need to persevere with patience for the Lord's perfect timing?

6. Choose a verse from today's study to be your memory verse for the week. Record it here and begin to memorize it today!

DAY 3 – BEGIN IN PRAYER

1. Read Nehemiah 2:1-10.

2. As Nehemiah did his best to serve the king with joy (he had never been sad in his presence), what observation did the king make? (v. 2)

How did Nehemiah react to the king's questioning?

In the days in which Nehemiah lived, it was never good to "rain on the king's parade." His broken heart having been discovered, Nehemiah became dreadfully afraid! What details do we find in Proverbs that give us a better picture of these dire circumstances?

   a. Proverbs 16:14

b. Proverbs 19:12

3. Holding his breath Nehemiah mentions Jerusalem, knowing full well past administrations had seen it as a rebellious city that was not to be rebuilt. What does he say to the king?

Nehemiah honestly shares the concerns of his heart with the king. He didn't give a big sales pitch or exaggerate the need; he simply laid out the details of the destruction of the city of Jerusalem. Perhaps he thought he was dead now for sure! What does Proverbs 21:1 teach us that will assist you when you find yourself facing a demanding king (or your boss, or some other authority in your life)?

4. What instruction and encouragement do we find regarding the importance of being obedient to the Lord's direction and will even in the face of opposition?

   a. Proverbs 29:25

   b. Isaiah 41:10

   c. Hebrews 13:6

In Acts 5:26-29 & 40-42, how did the disciples respond to the command of the council?

5. In Nehemiah 2:4, what was the king's response to Nehemiah's broken-heart?

Read the last part of Nehemiah 2:4 and the beginning of 2:5 together. Write it out below.

Sometimes we don't have time for long prayers! Notice that Nehemiah hadn't been trying to force his will or his timing on the king. He waited! He waited until God opened the door. We can be certain that he had spent many hours, days, and weeks in prayer. What are just a few of the promises we have to remind us that our

Heavenly Father longs for us to come to Him with the needs in our lives?

a. Jeremiah 33:3

b. John 15:7

c. Hebrews 4:16

d. James 1:5, 6

6. Record your memory verse for this week and spend time committing it to memory today. Remember the importance of hiding God's word it your heart!

DAY 4 – BEGIN IN PRAYER

1. Read Nehemiah 2:1-10.

2. In what was perhaps a very unexpected answer, the king asks Nehemiah two questions that only required one answer. What were his questions?

It is interesting that in parenthesis we gain the information that the queen was in attendance this day. We can only guess what difference this made. Maybe she had some influence, or maybe she gave him a nudge of approval! The important lesson to learn from observing Nehemiah this day is: He was prepared to answer the king's questions! You might say that he was pray-pared! What direction do you gain from the following Scriptures regarding our planning and God's direction in our lives?

a. Proverbs 3:5, 6

b. Proverbs 16:9

c. Psalms 32:8

d. Isaiah 48:17

3. We are not given the length of time Nehemiah estimated for the project. According to Nehemiah 5:14 he was gone over twelve years. We read in Nehemiah 2:6, so it pleased the king to send me. Have you experienced such a miracle in your life where the Lord opened a door when it seemed like it would have been impossible? If so, what was the circumstance?

What does Luke 18:27 say about seemingly impossible circumstances?

What is added in Luke 1:37 that you can apply to those "impossibilities" in your life?

What is the Lord's question to you today from Jeremiah 32:27?

4. Once the king had made the decision, Nehemiah said, I set him a time. He had an answer and a plan. This is quite different from those who say, "I am not making any plans, simply letting the Lord lead." Yet, walking by faith does not mean an absence of organization and planning. For four months Nehemiah had been planning by faith. In fact, had he not planned, he would have had no answers for the king's enquiries and might not have gotten to go at all. How does Luke 14:28-33 speak to the importance of diligent planning in the life of the believer?

What were Nehemiah's requests to the king? (v.7-8)

To Whom does Nehemiah give credit for this awesome turn of events?

5. This command given by King Artaxerxes, to restore and rebuild Jerusalem, is a very important event and date in our Biblical calendar. This commission to

Nehemiah is one anchor of a major prophecy that would establish all that God had planned for the nation Israel from that time forward, and it also gives us great insight and support for our understanding of the timeline of Revelation. Read Daniel 9:24-27 and record Daniel 9:25.

Note: If you desire further study on this prophecy in Daniel, Pastor Jack's in depth studies are available at www.growingthrugrace.com. The Product # for the Daniel 9 CD is 00TB277, or for MP3 it is 00TB277.mp3

6. Can you record your memory verse for this week without looking? If not, spend extra time working on it today!

DAY 5 – BEGIN IN PRAYER

1. Read Nehemiah 2:1-10.

2. The king's answer and his provision might have been more than Nehemiah could have ever imagined. He was granted approval for the journey back to Jerusalem and was given letters of safe passage through foreign lands and for all the timber that would be needed for the gates, the temple and his own home.

How would you describe God's gift of salvation and redemption that you have been granted by the King of Kings?

Personal: If you have not yet received the Lord Jesus Christ as your Savior, spend time today studying the following Scriptures in the Book of Romans and then, by all means, ask Him in – He is waiting for an invitation! Romans 3:10, 3:23, 5:12, 5:8, 6:23, 10:13, 10:9-10

3. How does the Bible describe the gifts that you have received as a child of the King of Kings?

   a. John 10:10b

   b. Psalm 36:7, 8

c. Ephesians 1:3-7

d. Ephesians 3:20, 21

e. Jude 24, 25

f. 1Peter 1:3-5

4. From the above Scriptures, make a list of the gifts and promises that you have in Christ Jesus.

Write a prayer of praise and thanksgiving to your Heavenly Father for all He has given you!

5. In Nehemiah 2:10 we are introduced to two men that will lead the opposition against Nehemiah and the work God had called him to accomplish. What are their names?

When you step out to serve God, you can be certain that opposition will arise! For Nehemiah the enemy was at first just two men – but the number would increase! We will study this topic in more detail in the following lessons but know this for sure - the enemy of your soul seeks your destruction and his mission is to keep you side-lined from the work. What does 1Peter 5:8 teach you about the tactic of your enemy?

What does Matthew 5:10-12, 20 say about the opposition to your faith and work?

6. Record your memory verse for this week without looking! Are you getting closer?

DAY 6 – BEGIN IN PRAYER

1. Read Nehemiah 2:1-10.

2. What lesson(s) from Nehemiah's life can you apply to your walk this week?

3. What are you praying about and planning for? What vision do you have for your life?

What seemingly "impossible" opportunities lay before you?

Are you expecting God to do great works and open doors?

What do you know for sure about those who oppose God's work in your life? Why?

4. Record your memory verse and reference without looking!

DAY 1 – BEGIN IN PRAYER

1. Read Nehemiah 2:11-20.

2. In Nehemiah 1 we learned that ministry is often born in the heart of an individual. The need will break your heart, your broken heart will lead you to fast and pray, which will bring you to a place where you will make yourself available to be used by the Lord. While Nehemiah waited for the Lord to open a door, he had wisely used that time in planning and praying. The opportunity presented to Nehemiah was more than he could ask or think and with the open door came the attacks of the enemy.

There is roughly a three-month gap between verses 10 and 11 of chapter 2. What did Nehemiah do on his first few days in Jerusalem?

Why do you think he kept God's leading to himself at this point?

When he began to share his vision, whom did he speak to?

What was his message?

What invitation did he extend to those he spoke to?

Who else heard the invitation to ministry given by Nehemiah but were not pleased? What were their responses to the call to serve?

How did Nehemiah react to his enemy's scorn and threats?

3. What lessons can you learn from this first reading of Nehemiah 2:11-20 that you will be able to apply in your walk with the Lord today?

DAY 2 – BEGIN IN PRAYER

1. Read Nehemiah 2:11-20.

2. Nehemiah takes the slow approach with great faith. He arrives in Jerusalem after four months of praying and planning, and perhaps as much as three months of traveling. Imagine the anticipation burning in Nehemiah's heart. He had never even seen the city of Jerusalem. He had only read of its majesty and glory, and then he heard the heart-breaking reports of its disrepair. You might think he would pull into town and begin to build! Instead, what did he do? Why do you think he waited?

Nehemiah needed to rest, gather his thoughts, assess the situation at hand, and seek the Lord for the next step. All too often when there is work to be done we just go for it without stopping to ask for the guidance and direction of the Lord. What instructions are we given in the following Scriptures that will help you to seek the Lord's direction before acting?

a. Psalm 25:8, 9

b. Proverbs 3:5, 6

c. James 1:5

3. Nehemiah set off on a secret night mission to see the work and to develop some ideas on how the Lord might want him to proceed. The quiet seeking of God is so needful in leadership. As the Lord calls us and we set out to serve him we must count the cost and be prepared to follow through to the end of the work. What exhortation are we given in Luke 14:28-33 that speaks to this important lesson?

What do the following verses add to this important topic of waiting?

a. Deuteronomy 4:29

b. Proverbs 8:17

c. Jeremiah 29:13

d. Matthew 7:7-11

4. It is absolutely vital in our walk with the Lord that we faithfully seek God by spending time in quietness where there is no other activity but prayer and waiting on Him. Why do you think this planning time is too often neglected in our lives?

What example are we given in Luke 6:12, 13 of the importance of seeking the Father's direction before we go forward to serve Him?

5. Nehemiah had seen God move mountains already; it would make no sense for him to change his methods now that he had arrived in Jerusalem. So while others slept, he was wide-awake seeking the will of God virtually by himself. A heart prepared before the Lord can go forth boldly and a leader can then give to others what he has received from God. We must first be students of the Word if we are going to be able to lead others in their walk with the Lord. What does 2Timothy 2:15 instruct us to do in preparation for serving?

6. Choose a verse from today's study to be your memory verse for the week. Record it here and begin to memorize it today!

DAY 3 – BEGIN IN PRAYER

1. Read Nehemiah 2:11-20.

2. Despite the great destruction, Nehemiah was not overwhelmed or discouraged for he knew God was faithful. God had, after all, brought him this far with miracle after miracle. Traveling around the perimeter Nehemiah saw areas where the rubble was piled so high he had to stumble across it on foot. Alan Redpath in Victorious Christian Living said, "When a real work of God is to be done, some faithful burdened servant has to take a long journey and weep in the night over the ruins." How do the following Scriptures remind you, that like Nehemiah, you have no need to fear when the task ahead of you seems impossible and overwhelming?

a. Deuteronomy 7:9

b. Lamentations 3:22, 23

c. 1Corinthians 1:9

d. Hebrews 10:23

e. 1Thessalonians 5:23, 24

3. Finally after four months of prayer, three months of travel, and three nights of reviewing the sad state of the walls of Jerusalem, it was time for Nehemiah to tell others what God had shown him. It was time for others to catch the vision and join the work! According to Nehemiah 2:17, what invitation did Nehemiah make to the leaders and the people of Jerusalem?

How did he assure them of the importance of the work and that the project would be successful? (v. 18)

What was the response of the people?

4. Nehemiah needed to share his vision and in doing so he gives us five important lessons to follow when we find ourselves as the leader of a project, a ministry, or a service team. These lessons are in verses 17 and 18. We will deal with two today and three in tomorrow's study. The first lesson is that Nehemiah identified himself with the problem. He did not blame the problem on others and he knew that he could not ask others to do what he himself was not willing to do! How is this lesson illustrated in the following Scriptures?

a. 1Timothy 4:12

b. 1Peter 5:2-5

c. John 13:13-15

5. The second lesson found in Nehemiah's example of sharing the vision and recruiting volunteers for the ministry is seen in the fact the he does not plead with, bargain or threaten the people. He was willing at each step to allow God to draw the hearts of the people. How does Zechariah 4:6 help you in the tasks you have been given to lead and accomplish?

6. Record your memory verse for this week and spend time committing it to memory today. Remember the importance of hiding God's word in your heart!

DAY 4 – BEGIN IN PRAYER

1. Read Nehemiah 2:11-20.

2. There must be a unity of vision in any ministry and a clear sharing of that vision from those in leadership if there is any hope of bearing much fruit. We cannot lead without a vision from the Lord that can be shared, or we will be working alone. What two lessons did we learn yesterday about sharing the vision we have been given?

   1.)

   2.)

3. The third valuable lesson that we can learn from studying Nehemiah's leadership skills is that when recruiting volunteers he appeals to their spiritual senses. In verse 17, why does Nehemiah encourage the people to come build the walls?

As believers, what is to be the motivation for our service to the Lord?

a. Ephesians 6:5-8

b. Colossians 3:17

c. Colossians 3:23

What awesome testimony is recorded about King Hezekiah in 2Chronicles 31:20-21 that ought to stand as a challenge to how we serve the Lord and how we lead others?

What does Ephesians 4:11-16 tell you about the spiritual strength of the Body of Christ and the responsibility of the members to do their part?

4. The fourth valuable lesson we can learn from studying Nehemiah is that Nehemiah doesn't offer rewards to the people to get help. How does Psalm 127:1 support the importance of following his example in our leadership?

What valuable words of exhortation did Joshua give to God's people in Joshua 22:5?

Personal: How well are you doing at obeying this important command?

David faced Goliath while all the armies of Israel were cowering in fear. David did not enter this battle for the rewards that King Saul was offering, but to bring glory to the True and Living God who Goliath was blaspheming. What declaration did David make in 1Samuel 17:45-47 just before he killed the giant?

Your love for the Lord must be the motivating factor in any service to Him! Any other motivation will eventually fail you or cause you to stop short of the goal. Our love is given and sustained by our abiding relationship with the Lord Jesus Christ. How does John 15:9, 10 describe the relationship between His love for us and our love?

According to 1John 3:17, 18, how will this abiding love show itself in our treatment of others?

5. The last lesson we can glean from watching Nehemiah share his vision is found in verse 18. We see that he faithfully shares what God had already accomplished in this matter. What does he tell the people in Nehemiah 2:18?

He did not ask the people to "join him" rather he asked them to "join in the Lord's work." What was the response of the people? (v. 18)

6. Can you record your memory verse for this week without looking? If not, spend extra time working on it today!

DAY 5 – BEGIN IN PRAYER

1. Read Nehemiah 2:11-20.

2. Nearly every step of victory in the book of Nehemiah is followed by a mention of opposition. What words of harassment and threat came from this increasing band of enemies? (v.19)

Look closely at Nehemiah's response! What did he say? What did he not say?

3. Nehemiah doesn't defend himself or his actions; rather he continues to trust in God alone. What encouragement do you find in Psalm 31:19 that will assist you when the enemy comes your way with attacks?

4. Nehemiah might have whipped out the king's letters, but he did not. Handling criticism well is vital for any Christian, especially those who would lead. Sometimes the criticism may come from an obvious enemy like these who were against Nehemiah's work. What are you to do when you face such criticism?

a. 1Corinthians 4:3-4

b. 1Peter 1:12-16

There are also times when the criticism comes from those closer to you and from whom you might not expect it. What lesson do you learn from this account of criticism in Mark 14:3-9?

How did the Lord quickly redeem this situation and how does it encourage you that He is always protecting you from unjust criticism?

5. In Matthew 5:10-12, what does our Lord Jesus Christ teach regarding criticism and the persecution of believers?

What further instruction are we given in the following Scriptures that will help us to not turn aside from the work because of the harsh words of the enemy or enemies?

a. Romans 16:17, 18

b. 2Timothy 3:1-5

c. Jude 1:17-21

6. Record your memory verse for this week without looking! Are you getting closer?

DAY 6 – BEGIN IN PRAYER

1. Read Nehemiah 2:11-20.

2. What lesson(s) from Nehemiah's life can you apply to your walk this week?

3. Make a list of the five points you learned from watching Nehemiah share his vision with the people. How will they help you as the Lord stirs you to His work and as you share the vision?

   1.)

   2.)

   3.)

   4.)

   5.)

4. Record your memory verse and reference without looking!

DAY 1 – BEGIN IN PRAYER

1. In this week's lesson our focus will be on two portions of the Book of Nehemiah that teach us another important lesson for those who are seeking to serve the Lord whole-heartedly. Read Nehemiah 2:10-20 and record the major events that occurred.

2. Read Nehemiah 4:1-12. Who appears again to try to hinder the progress of the work?

3. With these two portions of Scripture in mind, what can you expect when you step out to serve the Lord as He calls you?

4. Find a Scripture promise that reminds you not to focus on the opposition to God's work, but rather to keep your eyes on your Heavenly Father Who is able to overcome every enemy. Record the Scripture below and use it for your memory verse this week.

DAY 2 – BEGIN IN PRAYER

1. Read Nehemiah 2:10.

2. Even as Nehemiah was heading for Jerusalem with the blessings of King Artaxerxes and his full support, the news of what he was planning to do in Jerusalem had preceded him. Two men in particular did not welcome the news. What was their reaction to the news?

As believers, the single most important work God has for us is to share the Gospel with those who have not yet heard! But in doing so, we are guaranteed to run into the natural man. He is living in the kingdom of darkness. He is lost in his sin and resistant to the Word of God. As we seek to serve, the first type of opposition we face is, "Opposition by nature." Remember there are only two kingdoms – God's kingdom and the enemy's kingdom. How is the difference in these two kingdoms described by Paul as he stood before King Agrippa in Acts 26:17, 18?

3. Sanballat and Tobiah had only heard about Nehemiah's plans and they were up in arms. Why do you think they had such an attitude of prejudice?

Can you think of an example from your life when someone, knowing that you are a Christian, opposed you before they had ever spoken to you, or even met you?

What we often forget, as we daily walk in this world, is that we are firmly engaged in a war. It is a spiritual warfare. It is a war for souls. It is an eternal battle. How does John 10:10a describe the enemy against whom we fight?

What are the diabolical tactics of your enemy?

a. 2Corinthians 4:3, 4

b. Ephesians 2:2, 3

c. Ephesians 6:12

d. 1Peter 5:8

4. According to John 16:33, what are we guaranteed to face when we step out to reach the world with the love of Jesus Christ?

5. In Jesus Christ you have been given a new nature! You are a new person! You have a new heart! It is not so with those with whom you seek to share Jesus Christ. The enemy blinds them and they are trapped in the bondage of sin. Whenever you set out to serve the Lord, even before you put your hand to the task, EXPECT OPPOSITION! The root of this opposition is sin and the unredeemed old nature of man. They aren't opposed to you – they are opposed to Jesus Christ Who lives in and shines through you! How do the words of our Lord from John 15:18-21 encourage you today in the task He has set before you?

6. Record your memory verse for this week and spend time committing it to memory today. Remember the importance of hiding God's word in your heart!

DAY 3 – BEGIN IN PRAYER

1. Read Nehemiah 2:19, 20 and Nehemiah 4:1-3.

2. Now that we truly understand who the enemy is and what his plans are for us, we will take a closer look at some of the tactics he used against Nehemiah and which he will still employ against us today. By their very nature (unredeemed, in bondage, and blinded to the truth), those in the world will oppose your service for the Lord. One tactic they might utilize is opposing you by mockery. What has happened to the group of two in Nehemiah 2:19?

What did they say to Nehemiah?

How did Nehemiah respond to the laughing and mockery of these enemies?

What direction are we given about how we are to view the opposition by mockery that we face in our lives?

   a. Matthew 5:10-12

   b. Matthew 10:25, 26

   c. Luke 6:22, 23

3. In Nehemiah 4:1-3, we meet an ever-expanding group of opposition. The people had been making great strides in the work that God had first shared with Nehemiah. With the progress came increased attacks, with increased ammunition, and the use of all possible deterrents to the work. What were Sanballat and Tobiah saying and to whom were they saying it?

Often those the enemy is using to mock, laugh at, and despise the work of the Lord and his servants, do so by talking behind their back! These who mocked the work called the Jews feeble, the work impossible to finish, and the progress so incompetent that a fox could run up on the wall and knock it over. What modern day insults against Christians might fall under this category of the enemy's opposition?

What do the following Scriptures add to the subject of the opposition by mockery that is sure to come your way as you serve the Lord?

a. Mark 13:13

b. John 15:21

4. Satan will seek to mock our ideas, question our motives, point out our weakness and inabilities, and laugh at our zeal as mis-directed. Unfortunately, all too often this opposition works because no one likes to be ridiculed, or embarrassed, or made to be an outcast. What does Proverbs 29:25 say that reminds us that it should not be important to us what people think of us?

What is added in Matthew 10:28-33 that will give you boldness to not fear the mockery of the enemies in your life?

5. There is a fatal move within the church today to soften the preaching of the Gospel in order to attract people that may be offended by the Truth. It is clear that the preaching of the cross will bring division, but we must be careful never to succumb to the mockery, but rather boldly stand for the truth even if we stand alone. What does Paul write to Timothy in 2Timothy 4:16, 17 regarding a time he stood trial for preaching the Gospel?

6. Can you record your memory verse for this week without looking? If not, spend extra time working on it today!

DAY 4 – BEGIN IN PRAYER

1. Read Nehemiah 4:6-8

2. According to Nehemiah 4:6 half the work has already been completed. Obviously the angry feelings and the cutting remarks had done little to stop the forward progress of these believers in their quest of serving the Lord and re-building the wall. What does verse 6 tell us about the progress and the determination of the workers?

The enemy now tries a new and more intimidating attack. What had changed about this group of enemies and what was their new plan?

3. The numbers in the opposition party continued to increase. It is a fact that we can expect the attacks of our enemies to increase as our devotion and service to the Lord increases. The tactics of Nehemiah's enemies escalated. They went from mockery and insult to threat and intimidation. The critics would soon outnumber the laborers. The danger had gotten more personal. The cost of serving had become much more demanding and much more dangerous. How does Luke 14:25-35 speak about the cost of discipleship? What is required to truly follow?

What does Matthew 10:32-39 say that stands as a challenge for us to review the depths of our commitment to following the Lord?

4. Nehemiah's plight against his enemies ought to convince us that Satan in not interested in a fair fight. The word terrorist has come into sharp focus in our times. Not many in our country have been asked to give their lives for the

cause of Christ, but there are many countries today in which brothers and sisters in Christ are dying for proclaiming Jesus Christ as their Lord and Savior. Have you heard of someone who has given their life for their faith? Share and example if you can! Check out www.persecution.com.

Will you commit to pray for those who daily face threat and intimidation against their devotion and service for the Lord?

Record the words Jesus spoke to His disciples in Luke 9:23, 24?

What promise are we given in 2Timothy 3:12?

From 2Timothy 1:12, what was the Apostle Paul's conviction regarding the sure and certain suffering?

5. The question for us to answer as we study the Book of Nehemiah is, what if we were there? How would you respond? Would you keep building, or run and hide? We can practice dying to the smaller things in order to grow, so that if ever our lives are required we will not waver. Your on-going walk with Jesus that is shining brightly and seen by others may mean the death of your career, the death of a relationship, or the death of a friendship. You may have to walk away from a job, from a school, or even from your family, as we studied in the above Scriptures. What promise are we given by our Lord in Mark 10:29, 30?

What is recorded about the life of Moses in Hebrews 11:24-26? How does his decision encourage you in your walk today?

6. Can you record your memory verse for this week without looking? If not, spend extra time working on it today!

DAY 5 – BEGIN IN PRAYER

1. Read Nehemiah 4:10-12.

2. It seems that halfway finished is always a good time to become discouraged. Halfway through places us in a position to have forgotten the beginning excitement and enthusiasm and we cannot yet see the finish line. We start

asking, "why did we start, and will we ever finish?" It is at this point the enemy of our soul comes full force with a different type of opposition. He begins to oppose the work through discouragement and fear! How do Moses' words to the children of Israel in Deuteronomy 20:1-4 help you to remember Who will bring you victory against the enemies in your life?

What important lessons do we find in the following Scriptures that speak to the issue of fear?

a. Isaiah 41:10

b. Isaiah 43:1, 2

c. John 14:27

d. 2Timothy 1:7

3. Take note that the length of the work and the relentless onslaught of the opposition can become a tool in the hands of the enemy. (Nehemiah 4:10-12) Threats and intimidation planted thoughts of fear and discouragement. Who is it that is repeating the enemies' threats among the people of God?

What were their negative opinions about the work that remained?

What seeds of fear did they plant about the attacks of the enemy? (v. 11)

4. You will always find those with "little faith" who can give you ten reasons for not doing anything you believe God has placed in your heart. They might say it is too ambitious, too unrealistic, or too expensive...or the 10th excuse,

which always seems to be the same, we tried it before and it didn't work! How would obeying the following Scriptures help to strengthen your walk with the Lord and give you certain victory over your enemies today?

a. Isaiah 40:31

b. Hebrews 12:1-3

c. 1Corinthians 9:24

d. 1Corinthians 15:58

5. One theme that runs through the book of Nehemiah is that we are to continue to serve faithfully even when the work is constantly opposed by so many. What exhortation are we given in Galatians 6:7-9 that will redirect our focus from the opposition to the One who will carry us through to victory?

6. Can you record your memory verse for this week without looking? It is very important!

DAY 6 – BEGIN IN PRAYER

1. Read Nehemiah 2:10-20 and 4:1-12.

2. What lesson(s) from Nehemiah's life can you apply to your walk this week?

3. Make a list of the types of opposition we have seen Nehemiah's enemies use against Him, which your enemy will seek to use against you to sidetrack the work you are called to do for your Lord.

4. Record your memory verse and the reference without looking!

DAY 1 – BEGIN IN PRAYER

1. Read Nehemiah 3:1 – 4:9.

2. During this first reading of Nehemiah 3:1 – 4:9, what impression do you get about the importance of teamwork?

Did you notice that some people did not help? Who were they? Why do you think they did not take part in the rebuilding?

There are several references to the occupations of some of these workers. Why do you think it is important that we know the high priest, the priests, the goldsmiths, and the merchants all joined in the work?

Many labored close to their homes, why do you think this would have been important?

3. What lessons can you learn from this first reading of Nehemiah 3 – 4:9 that you will be able to apply in your walk with the Lord today?

DAY 2 – BEGIN IN PRAYER

1. Read Nehemiah 3:1 – 4:9. (Just one more time!)

2. Chapter 3 gives us a detailed account of the start of the wall-building project. It tells us who did what and where they did it. Except for a few proud elitists mentioned in verse 5, everyone seemed to have joined in to help from the smallest to the greatest. This list of names and what each individual was accomplishing is a great illustration of how God builds the church. In the Body of Christ everyone has a part; everyone is happy in the place that God has put them; and they have great respect for one another…this is how it is when we function like the Body of Christ should function. Record 1Corinthians 12:18 here!

According to 1Corinthians 12:18, who is it that assigns the position of the members in the Body of Christ?

3. What details about the unity of ministry within the body do we find in the following portions of Scripture? (Rather than write out the verse – tell what it means in practice and function within the church).

 a. 1Corinthians 12:19

 b. 1Corinthians 12:20 – 24a

 c. 1Corinthians 12:24b

 d. 1Corinthians 12:25, 26

4. The details of the work we see recorded in Nehemiah 3 are an awesome example of God's work amongst His people. Remember, it was a work that began with the faith of just one man – Nehemiah. A diligent, active, and faithful church is dependent upon, and traced to, a personal conviction of God in the heart of the individual. In other words, chapter 2 always precedes chapter 3 – a vision, a stirring, and then and a work to God's glory! It is vital that these steps always be followed. What exhortation was given to the Ephesian church in Revelation 2:3-5 when they placed their service before their devotion?

The work of building the wall made for some unusual labor teams. Priests, goldsmiths and rulers were mixing mortar and constructing the wall. They were laboring together and there was strength and encouragement in the teamwork! Can you give an example from Scripture showing how important it is that we serve together?

According to 1Peter 4:11, how are we to serve?

5. Some in Jerusalem missed out on the blessing of being involved in building the wall. Why do you think the nobles of Tekoa refused to serve?

There are those in the church who excuse themselves from serving by saying, "they are not called." Neither were many of these wall builders, as far as gifts are concerned. The important lesson we learn from this chapter is that there is a big difference between "ministry gifts" and a general calling to serve! Your specific gift does not exclude you from meeting a need in a different area when it arises. How are we to serve one another?

a. Mark 10:42-45

b. John 13:14, 15

c. 1John 3:16-18

Several of the builders were working near their own homes. This is the best place to start your ministry – your home is your first mission field. What instruction did Paul send to Timothy regarding the selection of Elders in the church in 1Timothy 3:4, 5?

6. Choose a verse from today's lesson and begin to commit it to memory!

DAY 3 – BEGIN IN PRAYER

1. Read Nehemiah 4:1-9.

2. Again we see that opposition follows progress! What happened when Sanballat heard that the people were rebuilding the wall?

Contrary to the old saying, "words will never hurt you," words do hurt and they hurt a lot. Satan often uses criticism and derision to discourage us from serving God. How will knowing and believing the following truths keep you from falling prey to the lying "words" of your enemy?

a. John 15:4, 5

b. 2Corinthians 12:9, 10

c. Philippians 4:13

d. Ephesians 6:10-13

3. Satan seeks to mock our ideas, question our motives, get us sidetracked, and challenge our commitment and zeal. He will bring up past failures, and point to our inabilities. How do the words of the Apostle Paul in 2Corinthians 3:1-6 encourage you to stand fast in the calling you have as an epistle of Christ to a lost world?

4. Put yourself in Nehemiah's shoes. He had spent eight months in prayer and preparation for the work, and it results in criticism. When we face criticism regarding the quality of our work or even the motives for our service, the core issue that has to remain in the fore-front of our hearts is Who are we serving and why are we serving. The way we are to serve is described in the following Scriptures. How are we to serve?

a. Colossians 3:23, 24

b. Ephesians 6:5-8

What further encouragement do you find in the following exhortations and promises that will help you today as you serve the Lord in the face of criticism?

a. Isaiah 40:29-31

b. Hebrews 10:35-37

5. In order for us to endure we must understand the difference between the

human point of view and God's point of view. Our vision of the work must come from the Lord and it cannot be dependent upon anything of this world! How does Isaiah 55:8, 9 describe God's ways?

6. Continue to work on your memory verse for this week. How much can you record without looking?

DAY 4 – BEGIN IN PRAYER

1. Read Nehemiah 4:1-9.

2. According to verses 4 and 5, what powerful action did Nehemiah take against his enemy?

What invitation, with promise, are we given in Jeremiah 33:3?

3. How then are you to view your trials and how will you work to view them as tools the Lord wants to use to draw you closer to Him and make your faith stronger?

How does 1Peter 2:19-23 encourage you to submit your life to God's will through the trials and persecution you face in your life?

According to 1Peter 2:18, who is Peter speaking to and how does this apply to your walk with the Lord?

How do the following Scriptures encourage you to pray in, and through, your trials?

a. Psalm 25:1-5

b. Psalm 61:1-4

c. Psalm 143:7-9

4. An important lesson we can learn from Nehemiah's prayer is that we can honestly share the depths of our hearts with the Lord. What emotion do you imagine is motivating Nehemiah's prayer?

How does he fight this battle?

Personal: How do you?

According to Romans 12:17-21, how are we to treat our enemies, and why?

What promise does Proverbs 15:1-2, 28 add to this important subject?

5. Nehemiah obediently took his enemies before the Lord in prayer and left them at His feet. What benefits do we have, as believers, according to Hebrews 4:15, 16?

Take a look at Nehemiah 4:6, after Nehemiah prayed, what did he do? What progress did the people make?

Nehemiah prayed and then he persisted in his work! Opposition has very little effect on the progress when the servants have a mind to work! In 2Timothy 4:7, 8, how does Paul describe the course of his life in his last letter to Timothy, his son in the faith?

Personal: How does this compare to how you are running the race? What needs to be improved? What needs to be removed that's hindering? Is there a sin that needs to be repented of and cast away? Will you make the needed changes today?

6. Continue to work on your memory verse for this week. How much can you record without looking?

DAY 5 – BEGIN IN PRAYER

1. Read Nehemiah 4:1-9.

2. Beginning in verse 7, a more sinister cloud now appears on the horizon. Make a list of the enemies who are opposing the work of Nehemiah and his people.

The enemy goes from ridicule to attack mode. They began gathering around the work, ready to attack from all sides! They would not be able to stage a full-scale war because the king had forbidden it, but this was more like terrorist threats. No one knew from where or when the next attack would come therefore, all were threatened. According to Nehemiah 4:8, what was the purpose of these threats?

What do we learn from 1Corinthians 14:33 about confusion in the Body of Christ?

What does James 3:14-16 teach us about the origin and source of confusion?

3. The goal of the terrorist threat is to create confusion and fear. The good news to the one who trusts Jesus Christ as Lord and Savior is that we have NOTHING to fear! The number of our days are secure and when this life is finished we will forever be with Jesus! How do the following Scriptures encourage you in your walk of faith today?

   a. Romans 8:14-16

   b. 2Timothy 1:7

   c. 1John 4:17-19

4. In addition to the lack of fear and confusion, we have been given an even greater gift! What is it and how are you personally doing at possessing this possession?

   a. John 14:27

b. Galatians 5:22, 23

c. James 3:17, 18

5. By reading Nehemiah 4:9 it seems for the first time Nehemiah's example of praying is grabbing the hearts of others. With the increase of persecution, comes the increase of personal devotion. At the height of the Roman persecution of the church 10,000 a day were being killed for their faith, yet it did not stop the Gospel from spreading. In fact, the witness of the martyrs brought many more to bold proclamation of their faith. What plan did the wall builder set in motion in the face of the terrorist threats?

These builder servants had a heart to pray and an eye to watch! How does their plan compare with the instructions we have been given in Mark 13:33?

6. Continue to work on your memory verse for this week. How much can you record without looking?

DAY 6 – BEGIN IN PRAYER

1. Read Nehemiah 4:1-9.

2. What lesson(s) from Nehemiah's life can you apply to your walk this week?

3. From Nehemiah 4:1-9, what methods of intimidation and persecution can you expect the enemy to use in your life?

How are you to specifically deal with these attacks of the enemy?

Personal: How would you rate your mind to work, your heart to pray, and your eye to watch? What do you need to improve?

4. Record your memory verse and the reference without looking!

DAY 1 – BEGIN IN PRAYER

1. Read Nehemiah 4:10-23.

2. What seems to be happening to the morale of the workers now that they have reached the mid-point in the work?

The discouragement the people felt was caused by the fear of constant threats. What was Nehemiah's solution?

Did Nehemiah quit working in order to fight against the enemy?

3. What lessons can you learn from this first reading of Nehemiah 4:10-23 that you will be able to apply in your walk with the Lord today?

DAY 2 – BEGIN IN PRAYER

1. Read Nehemiah 4:10-23.

2. It is certainly not easy to maintain your faith as you labor for the Lord while the enemy is constantly on the offensive to oppose and harass your work. The lesson is we are not to leave the work for the battle. Unfortunately, but not surprisingly, the people were becoming discouraged. What was the report of the work's progress according to verse 10?

How does Paul describe the pressure of the ministry in 2Corinthians 4:8-11?

The road on which we are called to travel as we serve the Lord is not an easy one! There are no promises of ease, comfort, or rest! Read Nehemiah 4:10 again and then go back and read Nehemiah 4:2. Whose words were God's people repeating?

3. In every work, especially a spiritual work, the halfway point is the hardest time. No doubt clearing out the debris from each section, in order to lay a

good foundation, was back breaking labor. According to Hebrews 12:1-4, what are we to do to keep from being overwhelmed and discouraged by the amount of work that remains to be accomplished in our lives?

What do the following Scriptures add that when heeded will keep our eyes off the rubble and on the might and power of our Lord?

a. 2Corinthians 4:16-18

b. Galatians 6:9

4. The strength of the laborers is failing was the report of the leaders. This can also be said of our Christian walks. In the early days of our salvation we are excited about everything in the Lord. Just as Nehemiah's people built the walls, we too must build upon the strong foundation of Jesus Christ in our lives, and this work takes time. Some spiritual changes happen quickly, others take longer and the progress seems way too slow! As a believer, you are in a battle and there is not, and will never be a cease-fire agreement. What exhortation to continue in faith is found in the following Scriptures?

   a. 1Timothy 6:11, 12

   b. James 1:2-4

5. Not only had the people lost their strength, they had also lost their vision, their heavenly vision. Their eyes were not focused on God, but on the rubble. The people cried out saying, "There is so much rubbish." They also lost confidence saying, "we are not able to build the wall." Satan's opposition to our spiritual growth takes many forms but has a single purpose. That purpose is to keep us from allowing the Holy Spirit to build the walls of our lives in Jesus Christ as His temple. How will Paul's encouragement to Timothy in 2Timothy 3:14-16 keep us from losing vision and confidence at the half-way point in the battle?

How do the promises in these verses help you adjust your focus back on Him in Whom you will find victory?

a. 1Corinthians 15:58

b. Jude 24, 25

6. Choose a verse from today's lesson and begin today to commit it to memory!

DAY 3 – BEGIN IN PRAYER

1. Read Nehemiah 4:10-23.

2. The enemy moves from sarcasm and jeers to making personal threats of terrorism and attack. The fact that the people lived close enough to the enemy to hear these threats first hand caused God's people to want to quit the work and run. Death could be waiting for them just around the corner, and it was not so easy any more to serve the Lord in this political climate. Sometimes at the mid-point in our walks we begin focusing on the work, the enemy, and the seemingly impossibilities, instead, where should our hope and trust be directed?

   a. Psalm 112:6-8

   b. Hebrews 13:6

   c. 1Peter 2:13-15

3. Unfortunately some of Nehemiah's people had become conduits for the enemy to spread his threats of pending doom. Notice that the people were saying, our adversaries said…and they told us ten times… The people of God were quoting and then spreading the words of the enemy. It is interesting that the people who lived closest to the enemy had the least confidence in God's work. How does this sad truth apply to the believer in the Body of Christ?

Spiritually speaking, what specifically can we do to be certain that we are not dwelling close to the enemy's camp?

4. What must we do to keep ourselves from falling into this trap of being a tool the enemy can use to disrupt the work of God?

   a. Matthew 5:6

   b. Matthew 6:33, 34

   c. Mark 12:29-31

   d. Ephesians 6:17, 18

5. There are many in church that live closer to the enemy than they do to the Lord. They can become a real stumbling block in the body, and a tool to promote the enemy's negative agenda. Remember, there is no neutral zone in our spiritual walk, either we are going forward serving in faith or slipping backward and possibly taking others with us! As a believer, how are you to run, and why?

   a. 1Corinthians 9:24-27

   b. Philippians 2:14-16

   c. Hebrews 12:1, 2

6. Continue to work on your memory verse for this week. How much can you record without looking?

DAY 4 – BEGIN IN PRAYER

1. Read Nehemiah 4:10-23.

2. According to verse 13, what changes did Nehemiah make to increase the security in and around the building project?

Reassigning work areas and taking some from building to guarding no doubt slowed the work for a time, but it did not stop it! Teamwork in the Lord was vital and everyone was dependent upon one another to finish the work. In the same manner, being an active part of a local body strengthens us, and those around us, and helps the work of God to go forward! How can you apply the truths of the following Scriptures to improve your ministry in the Body of Christ?

a. Proverbs 27:17

b. Ecclesiastes 4:9-12

c. Hebrews 10:23-25

3. With all the pressure Nehemiah was facing, with the fear in the camp, and with doubt and uncertainty of heart running rampant, notice Nehemiah's words in Nehemiah 4:14, he says, "I looked, and arose and said..." Where did he turn with his concerns?

Nehemiah took his troubles to the Lord and invited the Lord to handle them. What instruction are you given in the following Scriptures that will guide you during the times you face pressures that seem to overwhelm you?

a. Psalm 55:22

b. Psalm 62:8

c. Philippians 4:6, 7

d. 1Peter 5:6, 7

4. Many of us fail by placing our trust and dependence on people rather than looking up to the Almighty. What important truth did Nehemiah bring to the remembrance of his people?

We must first learn to look up in the face of trial, pressure, hardship, or threats. According to Psalm 42:5, what was the secret of the Psalmist that we can apply to our daily lives?

Most often the issue is not that we don't know, it is that we forgot! Read Psalm 103 slowly! Record one verse to carry with you today as a Psalm of Praise and to help you to remember that you are not alone in your walk.

5. To the builders in Jerusalem, who had returned from Babylon in spite of hardship and danger, everything dear to them depended upon the completion of the wall. The wall would protect them, so the work was worth the cost. The same is true in your walk with the Lord, it is worth the investment of time and labor to achieve spiritual victory. To neglect the building of the walls of your faith is to forego your peace, joy, and hope! What does Ephesians 2:19-21 teach you about the building project you are to diligently engage in?

What was the outcome of the enemies' threat on this occasion according to Nehemiah 4:15? How did remembering the Lord, great and awesome, affect the progress of the people's work?

6. Continue to work on your memory verse for this week. How much can you record without looking?

DAY 5 – BEGIN IN PRAYER

1. Read Nehemiah 4:10-23. (It's important!)

2. Beginning in verse 16 we see that the Lord had given Nehemiah a clear battle

plan! His motto – Don't stop the building for the battle! How did Nehemiah and the people accomplish the work?

As believers, we must be committed to the fight! The war is for souls – the enemy has been clearly defined. What is his goal?

a. John 10:10a

b. 1Peter 5:8

3. We must be diligent to clearly define the enemy! According to Ephesians 6:10-13, who is your enemy and how can you be certain to have victory?

Continuing in Ephesians 6:14-17, list each part of the Armor of God and tell how it will protect you from the attacks of the enemy.

#1

#2

#3

#4

#5

#6

What valuable offensive weapon are we given to assure victory in the battle? (v. 18)

4. Obviously battles will come, but they must never take us from the building. Building is more important than battling. The walls of our lives must go up if we are to be a witness to others. Sometimes in the face of the battle we are tempted to abandon our time in fellowship, neglect our prayer life, or quit on our study. In making these choices – the enemy has victory. How does Nehemiah give us the right balance between protecting ourselves from attacks and continuing the work?

How do the following Scriptures encourage you not to stop the building because of the battle?

a. Colossians 4:2-6

b. 1Thessalonians 5:6-8

c. 2Timothy 4:2-5

5. Since the work on the wall covered a large territory, Nehemiah developed a central call for help in case of emergency. If trouble broke out in any section, everyone would be summoned to come and stand together. What direction did Nehemiah give the people and what promise did he make to them? (v. 20)

Dire circumstances call for selfless devotion to serve one another! What drastic measures did Nehemiah and his people take to protect one another and yet continue the work that God had called them to do? (v. 22-23)

How are we called to serve one another in the Body of Christ?

a. John 13:13-17

b. Romans 15:1-4

c. Galatians 6:1, 2

6. Continue to work on your memory verse for this week. How much can you record without looking?

DAY 6 – BEGIN IN PRAYER

1. Read Nehemiah 4:10-23. (Last time – for now!)

2. What lesson(s) from Nehemiah's life can you apply to your walk this week?

3. Give an example of a time when the attacks of the enemy caused you, or tempted you, to stop doing those important things that build the wall of faith in your life. What did you do?

What will you do differently, this time, if anything?

Personal: How is the balance between wielding the sword and the wall building in your walk today? Remember the enemy would have you quit the work! Re-read Nehemiah 4:14 and 20 and record a prayer of commitment today. Put on the whole armor of God…

4. Record your memory verse and the reference without looking! (It's important!)

DAY 1 – BEGIN IN PRAYER

1. Read Nehemiah 5:1-13.

2. According to this portion of Nehemiah, what new method of attack did the enemy bring against the people of God?

What action did Nehemiah take and what was the end result of his leadership?

3. What lessons can you learn from this first reading of Nehemiah 5:1-13 that you will be able to apply in your walk with the Lord today?

DAY 2 – BEGIN IN PRAYER

1. Read Nehemiah 5:1-13.

2. The tactic of destruction we will be studying this week is one of our enemy's greatest, and most effective, tools. In Nehemiah's day it almost ruined the project – sadly, this attack has not only damaged, but it has also destroyed many church fellowships, and continues to do so today. Where did this attack come from?

What is the crisis that caused the division amongst the people?

3. Internal dissention and strife in the camp led to everyone choosing sides, which certainly hindered, if not stopped, the progress of the wall building. For a time, Satan was winning. It is far too easy for the Body of Christ to lose sight of the fact that we are one in Jesus. We are not to be competing with other ministries, or other believers, but rather working for the same common goal. What does Galatians 5:14, 15 teach us about our responsibility to others in the Body of Christ?

What further instruction are we given in the following Scriptures regarding internal dissention in the Body of Christ?

a. Galatians 5:26

b. James 3:14-16

c. James 4:1-3

4. The crisis of the famine and the sacrifices of the labor had placed a great strain on many of the people. Large families had difficulty feeding everyone and the situation had turned desperate. High taxes and corruption from the tax collectors added even more to the burden. As a result, the people were being enslaved for their inability to pay, lands were being seized, and even children were sold into slavery. The worst part of it was that it was their Jewish brethren who were executing these injustices. People who fall into the trap of looking out for self, or seeking power, prestige, or personal gain cause division in the Body of Christ. A true disciple avoids these pitfalls. How ought we to live and relate to others in the body?

   a. Mark 8:34, 35

   b. Proverbs 13:10

   c. Philippians 2:3-5

   d. Philippians 2:14, 15

5. What was Nehemiah's response to the strife and infighting that was taking place amongst the people?

The people who were exploiting their brethren were clearly acting against God's instruction for the behavior of His children. How were they supposed to deal socially and financially with one another?

   a. Exodus 22:25-27

b. Leviticus 25:35-37

c. Deuteronomy 23:19, 20

6. Choose a verse from today's lesson and begin today to commit it to memory!

DAY 3 – BEGIN IN PRAYER

1. Read Nehemiah 5:1-13.

2. Nehemiah, like any great leader, became very angry when he heard the outcry of his people. Take careful note, what is the very first thing we are told that he does? (v. 7)

A very important trait of a wise leader is to be slow to anger, and slow to speak. Nehemiah did not rush out in anger to confront the nobles and leaders. Instead, he stopped to think it through. Since we have seen his track record for seeking the Lord in prayer, we can assume he sought the Lord's direction here. What vital instruction do we get from James 1:19, 20 that we must apply when there is conflict to be dealt with in our lives?

3. In speaking to the nobles and rulers regarding their sin, Nehemiah risked losing their support for the work, however, true spiritual victory comes in pleasing God, not in pleasing men. What testimony did Paul have among the church at Thessalonica according to 1Thessalonians 2:4-7?

It is inevitable that conflict will arise in serving, even within the church. How did Paul instruct Timothy to deal with this conflict according to 2Timothy 2:24-26?

4. After thinking the circumstance through, with prayer, what decision did Nehemiah make and what action did he take? (5:7)

What questions did he pose to these powerful men who were walking in sin?

Nehemiah clearly and publicly exposed the sin of these men! Why do you think this was necessary?

How do Paul's actions toward Peter in Galatians 2:11-14 compare with Nehemiah's confrontation with these powerful men in Jerusalem?

What further instruction does Paul give to his son in the faith, Timothy?

a. 1Timothy 5:19, 20

b. 2Timothy 4:2, 3

5. According to verse 9, what should be our main motive for walking in obedience to God's will and His Word?

What do you think it means to "fear God?"

To the unbeliever, the fear of God implies terror due to their separation from Him, but to the believer the fear of God is an awesome respect and reverence that brings us to worship. What do the following Scriptures add to your definition of fearing God?

a. Proverbs 1:7

b. Proverbs 9:10

c. Acts 9:31

d. 1Peter 2:17

6. Continue to work on your memory verse for this week. How much can you record without looking?

DAY 4 – BEGIN IN PRAYER

1. Read Nehemiah 5:1-13.

2. Nehemiah had the power and authority to tax the area for this building project, but he chose not to do so, trusting God instead. It seems that he was personally giving to help relieve the suffering of some of his brethren. He faced this current attack of the enemy head on, confronting those who were sinning against their brethren, instructing them on the steps they needed to take to cure the problem. The cure was a four-step answer that we can, and must, practice when we find that the sin of division has taken root in our lives. Step one is found in verse 10, what is Nehemiah's simple first step?

When we are convicted of sin the cure is to stop it! We cannot excuse our behavior by pointing to the past, giving excuses, or pretending the sin does not exist. We must call sin – sin and by prayer and the power of the Holy Spirit turn away from it in repentance. What encouragement do you gain from the following Scriptures on this subject?

a. Isaiah 1:16-19

b. Acts 3:19

c. 1Peter 3:10-12

d. 3John 11

Personal: Is there an area in your life where sin has been allowed to make itself at home? Will you willingly take this first step and choose to stop it! As you daily commit this area to the Lord, He is able to empower you to resist future temptations!

3. We find step number two in verse 11 of Nehemiah 5. Repentance is the first step, but in many cases of sin something more must take place. What does Nehemiah instruct us to do once we have recognized sin and repented of it?

How does this man's story recorded in Luke 19:1-10 illustrate this second step in Nehemiah's cure?

4. Step number three has to do with when the restitution takes place. What instruction did Nehemiah give regarding the time frame for action in verse 11?

To delay when God speaks to you is to allow time to dull the sharp edges of God's reproof. How does Matthew 5:23, 24 speak of the urgency of restoration among the brethren?

Record Hebrews 3:7, 8 asking the Lord to reveal any area that needs cleansing in your life TODAY.

5. Lastly, Nehemiah tells his people, and us his readers, that there is one final step that must be taken in conjunction with the first three. Whom did Nehemiah summon and why?

He commanded the people to make this promise, this vow, to the Lord and not to him. Repentance is indeed an oath before God acknowledging that we are willing and desirous for His work of sanctification in our lives. What command is given to us in Hebrews 12:1, 2 and how will you apply it to your walk with the Lord today?

6. Continue to work on your memory verse for this week. How much can you record without looking?

DAY 5 – BEGIN IN PRAYER

1. Read Nehemiah 5:1-13.

2. Nehemiah asks God to deal with those who might still be unwilling to follow God's will for His community in Jerusalem. What was the response of the people to Nehemiah's four-step restoration plan?

Bound to the Lord by word and promise the congregation rejoices with a heartfelt Amen! Obedience will cause joy for us and for those in and around our lives. What does Psalm 133:1 tell us about this unity that is of absolute importance in the Body of Christ?

3. In Jerusalem the work would now proceed and the enemy was once again defeated by the faithful obedience of the people to God's Word! We, too, must be a stepping-stone and not a stumbling block as we seek to be a part of the work of God in the body of Christ. What exhortation is given to us in Romans 14:12, 13?

4. If an issue of division arises between you and someone else in the body, how must you handle it according to Matthew 18:15?

If the matter cannot be resolved in this private manner, what are you to do next? (Matthew 18:16, 17)

5. What more do you learn from the following Scriptures about the importance of unity in the Body of Christ?

   a. Proverbs 25:8-10

   b. Mark 9:50

   c. Romans 12:17-21

d. Colossians 3:12, 13

e. 1Peter 3:8

Choose one of the above Scriptures, write it out on a separate sheet of paper, and carry it with you for the next week. When an issue of contention begins to arise, refer to the instructions in this verse and see how the Lord will be able to guide your actions accordingly!

6. Continue to work on your memory verse for this week. How much can you record without looking?

DAY 6 – BEGIN IN PRAYER

1. Read Nehemiah 5:1-13.

2. What lesson(s) from Nehemiah's life can you apply to your walk this week?

3. What four necessary and practical steps did Nehemiah lay out for us that you will be able to use the next time the enemy attempts to attack your family, your friends, or your church with the tools that divide from within?

   1.

   2.

   3.

   4.

4. Record your memory verse and the reference without looking! (It's important!)

DAY 1 – BEGIN IN PRAYER

1. Read Nehemiah 5:14-19.

2. How many years did Nehemiah serve as governor?

What did he do very differently than his predecessors?

Why did he make this decision?

Review Nehemiah 5:8-13 to be reminded of the circumstances of the people during the times in which Nehemiah was ruling. What was taking place?

3. What lessons can you learn from this first reading of Nehemiah 5:14-19 that you will be able to apply in your walk with the Lord today?

DAY 2 – BEGIN IN PRAYER

1. Read Nehemiah 5:14-19.

2. In our text this week we find Nehemiah's personal life on display. We are given a rare insight into the private dealings of a man in charge. It is a model for all who would seek to be used by God to lead others. The external trials and persecution against Nehemiah's ministry had definitely been hard to endure, but there is another grave test of our faith. What do you think this test might be?

Nehemiah had been the servant of a king and now he finds himself the governor of Jerusalem wielding a tremendous amount of power. Can you think of any other men or women from the Bible who experienced similar advancement and did so with integrity and honor?

What wise counsel does the Psalmist Asaph offer in Psalm 75:5-7 that we would do well to follow carefully?

3. Nehemiah accepts this high position of governor from the king and sees it immediately as a place from which he can serve the Lord. Promotion brings us greater opportunity, but it also brings greater accountability and tempting privileges. What does 1 Chronicles 4:9, 10 teach us about the heart's desire of an honorable man named Jabez?

4. What instructions and warnings do we receive from the following Scriptures regarding how we are to live and how we are to serve when advancement comes or riches increase?

   a. Psalm 62:10-12

   b. Matthew 7:12

   c. Luke 12:15

   d. Ephesians 6:9

   e. Colossians 4:1

5. Nehemiah remembered the very day he was made the governor, he recalled the years he had served and was able to make comment on his response to the benefits he might have enjoyed in this high position. Food allowances were available, but Nehemiah refused taking liberties with his expense account. With privilege, the enemy can often bring a very subtle temptation to sin. What lessons do we learn from the account of the unfaithful servant in Matthew 24:45-51?

According to Luke 9:46, what issue of temptation continued to occur even amongst the disciples, as they walked with the Lord?

What was Jesus' response to this dispute? (Luke 9:47, 48)

6. Choose a verse from today's lesson and begin to commit it to memory!

DAY 3 – BEGIN IN PRAYER

1. Read Nehemiah 5:14-19.

2. Nehemiah could have followed the former governors' practices of overtaxing the people to enrich himself, demanding they pay tribute of bread, wine, and silver, and arguing that this is how it has always been done! But instead he chose to be above reproach and not give the enemy a foothold. For Nehemiah, a leader who honored the Lord first, promotion gave opportunity to bring about change. What was it that kept Nehemiah from following the example of the former leaders?

What do you remember from last week's study about the Biblical definition of the fear of God?

3. How do the following Scriptures add even more depth to your understanding of the fear of God, and how will they affect your walk with the Lord today?

   a. 2Samuel 23:3

   b. Psalm 36:1

   c. 2Corinthians 7:1

   d. Ephesians 5:18-21

4. Nehemiah did not choose to walk in the status quo, but rather to rise above it! He declared, even the former governors' servants bore rule over the people, but I did not do so... Sometimes we, as believers, must say more and say it more often because of the times in which we live. Refusing to follow custom or tradition, Nehemiah sought to do only what God desired for his life. What instruction are we given regarding how we ought to conduct ourselves as believers in a dark world?

a. Romans 12:1-3

b. Ephesians 4:1-3

c. Ephesians 4:17-20

d. 1Peter 1:13-16

5. It is much easier to follow the crowd than to set the pace. The Lord is looking for men and women who will be fully committed to obeying His Word, regardless of the pressure or opinions of others. What important truth do you learn from Psalm 24:3-5?

Therefore, we are to live for Him and set the standards for others to follow instead of following along and excusing ourselves with the old saying, "everyone is doing it." What promise is given to those who love and keep God's Word in John 14:23?

6. Continue to work on your memory verse for this week. How much can you record without looking?

DAY 4 – BEGIN IN PRAYER

1. Read Nehemiah 5:14-19.

2. Nehemiah was not diverted from the task that had brought him to Jerusalem. The passion of his heart was to see the walls of Jerusalem rebuilt in order to bring honor to the LORD and security to His people. What point does he make in verse 16 that illustrates a singleness of heart?

Nehemiah used his position to move closer to the goal God had set: building the walls! He was not sidetracked with land acquisition or expansionism. He stayed on track and so did those who served with him – his staff shared his focus. What example do we find in the following Scriptures that illustrate the importance of staying the course?

a. Luke 10:42

b. Philippians 3:13, 14

c. 1Corinthians 9:24-27

3. A true leader has others following, and a true spiritual leader must clearly define the course of direction, and the goals and objectives of the Christian walk. Nehemiah's life had taken a dramatic turn and the added responsibility demanded diligence and continued focus. The true spiritual leader leads by example. What instruction did the Apostle Paul give in 1Corinthians 11:1 to those who were following him?

Personal: Whom are you inviting to serve the Lord Jesus Christ in the same manner that you are? If this question is hard to answer, will you ask the Lord to make the necessary changes in your heart and life so that you can confidently invite others to "follow you?"

4. The world often places higher standards on Christians than we do on ourselves. We are expected, because of our faith in Christ, to live a totally different life. The world watches you closely because if what you believe is true, how you live will differ greatly from those who do not trust Jesus. All too often, in practice, there is very little difference. According to the following verses, what are the differences between the life of the believer and the life of the unbeliever?

a. Psalm 1:1-6

b. 2Corinthians 6:14-17

5. What a joy it must have been for Nehemiah to be able to have a testimony of honest godliness as he served the Lord in this position of power. Promotion and success bring greater accountability and privileges, and it provides an opportunity for positive change. How are you to live and lead those in your life?

   a. Romans 13:12-14

   b. Ephesians 5:7-11

   c. 1Peter 2:9-12

6. Continue to work on your memory verse for this week. How much can you record without looking?

Day 5 – Begin in Prayer

1. Read Nehemiah 5:14-19.

2. Nehemiah found himself personally caring for 150 people. Another lesson we learn from studying Nehemiah's life is that promotion demands a cost if the work is to last. Nehemiah put his money where his mouth was. He paid the cost to see God work. He was willing to experience personal sacrifice in order to assist in God's work and to protect God's children. According to Luke 14:27-33, what type of commitment is required of the disciple?

3. Nehemiah paid a hefty personal cost, but he was glad to help since the burden on his people was so heavy. What instruction is given in 1Timothy 6:17-19 about how we are to use the provision that God has given us?

4. What more do you learn regarding God's provision and your responsibility to the people the Lord puts in your life?

    a. Psalm 62:10

    b. Luke 6:35

    c. Galatians 6:9, 10

    d. Hebrews 6:10

    e. Hebrews 13:16

5. Nehemiah was only interested in God's approval of his heart and actions. What is his plea in Nehemiah 5:19?

Record Colossians 3:23, 24 here and use these verses as the motivation for whatever you do today – if God is pleased with your heart and actions, it doesn't matter what others think! Amen!

6. Continue to work on your memory verse for this week. How much can you record without looking?

DAY 6 – BEGIN IN PRAYER

1. Read Nehemiah 5:14-19.

2. What lesson(s) from Nehemiah's life can you apply to your walk this week?

3. Nehemiah teaches us that if we want to serve and be promoted to the place of greatest usefulness for God and His kingdom, we must serve willingly, live a life above reproach, focus on pleasing God alone, and setting the standards for others to follow! How are you doing? What area is in need of improvement?

4. Record your memory verse and the reference without looking! (It's important!)

DAY 1 – BEGIN IN PRAYER

1. Read Nehemiah 6.

2. One thing Nehemiah teaches us is that serving the Lord requires a real persistence of faith, for the road is not an easy one to walk. In chapter 6, the enemy returns with another attack on the work. How is this one somewhat different than the ones that came before?

Why might this type of attack be very effective if it was successful?

3. What lessons can you learn from this first reading of Nehemiah 6 that you will be able to apply in your walk with the Lord today?

DAY 2 – BEGIN IN PRAYER

1. Read Nehemiah 6.

2. Up to this point in the project the work of God in Jerusalem had moved forward fairly quickly even against heavy opposition, which included mockery, threats, internal strife, and personal attacks, which had all failed. This time the attack would come against the leader, and it was personal and direct. The enemy had decided to try to stop the work from the top. What was the enemy's request?

What was Nehemiah's response?

Why wouldn't he go meet with the enemy?

3. The climax to the book of Nehemiah is not the result that we see here in Nehemiah 6:15 – the wall was complete. God had a much greater vision for the lives of Nehemiah and his people (and for us too)! God was building faith, true genuine faith, in the hearts of those who chose to follow Him in Jerusalem. Too often we see faith as receiving, but by Biblical definition faith is waiting on God. What do we learn about faith from Hebrews 11:1 and Hebrews 11:6?

4. Satan's attack here is interesting, it seems to be a last ditch effort coming on the heels of a ribbon-cutting ceremony. The enemy of your soul never rests, and we cannot be surprised by his attacks even in our victories. In Nehemiah's life the enemy resurfaces, this time with a different tactic all together: let's be friends! Some might have thought Nehemiah was too callous in his response, but discernment from the Lord is vital. What do we learn about walking in discernment and seeking the Lord for our every step?

   a. Proverbs 14:15

   b. Matthew 10:16

   c. 2Corinthians 11:13, 14

   d. Ephesians 5:15-17

Nehemiah knew that his enemies had not repented of their wickedness and he sensed trouble. Also, he knew that leaving the work was not an option. What do the following Scriptures teach us about being on guard against such an "invitation" from our enemy?

   a. John 15:19

   b. 1John 2:15-17

   c. James 4:4

5. Perhaps the pressure was quite strong amongst Nehemiah's staff to "make peace." Yet Nehemiah stood firm! As believers, we must refuse to compromise the truth, even for "so-called" peace. So Nehemiah sent messengers to them, saying, I am doing a work, so that I cannot come down. Why should the work cease while I leave it and go down to you? Why had the city had so many years of sorrow and no wall? Distractions! Distraction is a very effective tool of the enemy. According to James 4:6, 7, how can we defeat him?

Personal: Is there something God has been calling you to do that you began, but then became distracted? Are there changes you vowed to make, but didn't follow through on? Will you commit today to putting Jesus, your relationship with Him, and the work He has called you to do, above all else? If so what "invitations" from the enemy need to be declined this week?

6. Choose a verse from today's lesson and begin to commit it to memory!

DAY 3 – BEGIN IN PRAYER

1. Read Nehemiah 6.

2. Since the enemy's Plan A didn't work – "won't you be my neighbor," the enemy needed to move on to Plan B. After sending four personal letters of invitation that were all rejected, what was Sanballat's next tactic?

Why do you think that he might have chosen this form of communication?

3. The fifth letter was an open letter to be read publicly. The kindness of the enemy was wearing thin, and his true heart was revealed. This letter was filled with slander and blackmail. Lies, slander, and gossip are from the rumor factory of hell. What do you learn about this sin of the lips and how will being reminded that the Lord hates it help to guard your tongue this week?

   a. Exodus 20:16

   b. Psalms 101:5

   c. Proverbs 6:16-19

   d. Proverbs 10:18, 19

What instruction is given in Ephesians 4:29 about the use of your tongue?

4. Notice that rumors and lies rarely have a source. Nehemiah 6:6 says, it is reported among the nations... According to Nehemiah 6:8, 9, what two steps did Nehemiah take in response to the slander and blackmail?

   1.

   2.

Nehemiah's response was a firm denial! He declared it to be a lie of their own invention. The goal of the enemy was to create fear. When your enemy comes with this tactic, how does Psalm 31:13-20 encourage you in your faith?

Read and meditate on Isaiah 41:10-13. Record your own prayer of trust and praise to Jesus, your Lord and Savior.

5. Nehemiah admits to being scared, yet he faithfully clings to the LORD, and he stands firm against the attacks. As the intensity of the personal attacks increase in our lives, what are we to do as believers in Jesus Christ?

   a. Romans 12:17-21

   b. 1Corinthians 4:1-5

6. Continue to work on your memory verse for this week. How much can you record without looking?

DAY 4 – BEGIN IN PRAYER

1. Read Nehemiah 6. (No skipping this reading – it's important!)

2. Pretense of friendship had failed and so had slander: the next plot (Plan C) was the tactic of coming as a wolf in sheep's clothing. Who was Shemaiah and what counsel did he give to Nehemiah?

Satan is far more dangerous as an angel of light than as a roaring lion. In 2Corinthians 11:12-15, what does Paul say regarding those who tormented the early church from within?

3. So Shemaiah, under the guise of being a prophet of God, comes with a word "from the Lord," but he was on the enemy's payroll. His advice – Run and hide! Protect yourself at all costs! What would have happened to the work if Nehemiah followed this advice?

What happened to the Apostles in Acts and how did they respond to the verbal threats and the physical mistreatment?

a. Acts 4:16-20

b. Acts 5:40-42

4. Your enemy will often try to work through the feigned inspiration of those who oppose the work that God has called you to do. Sometimes the threat will be from within, as sheep in wolves' clothing, sometimes from those who call you "friend," and sometimes directly from the enemy. In any case, how do the following Scriptures strengthen your resolve not to stop the work God has given you to do?

a. Isaiah 8:12, 13

b. Isaiah 51:6-8

c. Matthew 10:17-20

d. Matthew 10:28-31

e. Romans 8:35-39

5. What was Nehemiah's response to Shemaiah's advice?

What did the Lord reveal about Shemaiah's motives?

Nehemiah understood who he was in the Lord, he knew Who he was serving, and he was not so afraid that he had gotten out of touch with God by focusing on the enemy and his lies. Fear can cause irrational behavior. What promise is given to us in 2Timothy 1:7 that, when applied to the threats of the enemies in your life, will bring you victory?

In Nehemiah 6:14 how does Nehemiah deal with the fear and the threats of the enemy? Are you willing to follow his example today?

6. Continue to work on your memory verse for this week. How much can you record without looking?

DAY 5 – BEGIN IN PRAYER

1 Read Nehemiah 6.

2. In the midst of this onslaught of persecution from the enemy, the wall was finished in 52 days. It had been in ruins for over 160 years, but here, by God's grace it stands completed! It was humanly impossible. What does Mark 10:27 teach us about accomplishing the impossible?

How do the following Scriptures add to your understanding of the unlimited power of your Heavenly Father?

a. Jeremiah 32:27

b. Luke 1:37

c. Hebrews 7:24, 25

3. How did the finished wall affect the enemy around Nehemiah?

What did they conclude about the wall?

In spite of the difficulty we face, we can be certain that Satan will be defeated, and that God will turn the hardship of the trial for good. What do you learn about this important truth that will strengthen your resolve today?

a. 1Corinthians 15:58

b. Philippians 1:12-14

c. Romans 8:28

4. We can thank God that He does not call us to initiate programs for Him, but rather He is simply looking for faithful vessels that He can use in all situations. Don't be discouraged, and never give up, for one day the enemy will bow! Record Psalm 126:5-6 and spend a few minutes thinking about this truth in regards to your battles with the enemies in your life!

5. For Nehemiah, even with the wall complete, the persecution continued. What did the enemy do now?

When we sow in the Spirit, even in tears, the fruit will eventually come forth. If it means planting in opposition, at great personal cost, or even without much assistance, we can be certain that we are not alone in our labor. The important lesson to learn, and remember, from Nehemiah's life is that Satan wants to keep you from planting and he will try just about anything to keep you out of the Word, out of church and away from serving. What does Hebrews 10:35-39 say about the necessity of endurance?

6. Continue to work on your memory verse for this week. How much can you record without looking?

DAY 6 – BEGIN IN PRAYER

1. Read Nehemiah 6.

2. What lesson(s) from Nehemiah's life can you apply to your walk this week?

3. In what ways have you seen the enemy extend an invitation of "friendship" to the church?

What are some "distractions" of the world that commonly compromise our service to the Lord?

4. Record your memory verse and the reference without looking! (It's important!)

DAY 1 – BEGIN IN PRAYER

1. Read Nehemiah 7-8.

2. Chapters 1-6 gave us the account of the reconstruction of the walls of Jerusalem under the leadership of Nehemiah over a 52-day period in 445BC; the remaining portion of the book of Nehemiah (7-13) will deal with the retraining of the people. The focus will shift in part from Nehemiah to Ezra, the scribe and priest, who'd been in Jerusalem 13 years longer than Nehemiah. In captivity, most of the Hebrews had lost their ability to read and write Hebrew. The title of this lesson is, Steps to Personal Revival. From this first reading what steps do you see the people taking that led to their recommitment to the LORD?

3. What lesson(s) can you learn from this first reading of Nehemiah 7-8 that you will be able to apply in your walk with the Lord today?

DAY 2 – BEGIN IN PRAYER

1. Read Nehemiah 7.

2. With the wall and the gates finished, steps are now instituted to protect the city's inhabitants. What were those steps?

Who was placed in charge?

How does Nehemiah describe the character of Hananiah the leader of the citadel?

3. Read 1Timothy 3:8-13. How does the description of Hananiah, the leader of Jerusalem security, compare with Paul's instruction to Timothy regarding the spiritual qualifications of deacons in the church?

Use your Dictionary of Bible Words to define the word deacons from 1Timothy 3. Why is it so important that those who serve the Body of Christ be held to such high standards?

Find one or two Bible verses that support your answer to the last question. What are they?

4. Guards were set up at the gates and security was in place to protect the people, but according to Nehemiah 7:4 what was the condition of the city within the walls of Jerusalem?

What was Nehemiah's next course of action and why did he do what he did? (v. 5)

Nehemiah tells us that God again spoke to his heart. He was to begin to put in order the practice of worship and service at the Temple. Nehemiah was open to hear from God and obedient to obey as the LORD instructed. By what methods does God speak to those who love and follow Him today?

How do the following Scriptures support or add to your answer?

a. Hebrews 1:1-3

b. Psalm 19:7-11

c. John 14:26

d. Romans 10:17

e. 1Corinthians 2:12-16

f. Ephesians 4:11-16

5. Nehemiah found a register of the genealogy of those who had come up in the first return with Zerubbabel and Joshua in 536BC. The total number of people listed here in Nehemiah is 49,942 and then there was an additional 2000 families who returned to Jerusalem with Ezra in 457BC. Since the LORD often includes detailed information in His Word of the names and the numbers of individuals, what can we learn about the importance of our lives, even when we feel insignificant compared to the vastness of His plan?

Record Psalm 139:17, 18 and ask the Lord to remind you often today of the price He was willing to pay to give you intimate access to the holiness of His presence! Selah!

6. Choose a verse from today's lesson and begin today to commit it to memory!

DAY 3 – BEGIN IN PRAYER

1. Read Nehemiah 8.

2. Beginning here in Nehemiah 8 we have the first recorded spiritual revival in Jerusalem since their return from captivity in Babylon 91 years earlier. It is interesting to note that true Biblical revivals always begin with believers, not with unbelievers. Revival most often happens when God's Word thrills older saints again and they seek to know Him better and follow Him more obediently. He, then, ignites their hearts with a new passion and desire to reach the lost with the Good News of salvation. Jerusalem had a wall outside, but no life inside. It was a structure without a heart! How did this revival begin?

According to Revelation 2:1-4, how might the church of Ephesus resembled Jerusalem with her walls intact without true worship?

How can this tragic circumstance take place in the heart of the individual believer? According to Revelation 2:5, what are we to do if we find ourselves in this backslidden state?

3. Revival takes place when the church returns to God's Word and commits to submit to its authority. Today, not unlike many other generations, there are those within the church who are turning away from total dependence upon the transforming, saving power of the Scriptures, and are employing the methods of the world to try to influence change in the lives of the people who come to them. What do you learn about the absolute necessity of our total submission to, and adherence upon, the Word of God?

   a. Proverbs 30:5

   b. Matthew 24:35

   c. Romans 1:16

   d. Ephesians 6:17

   e. 1Peter 1:22-25

4. The first day of the 7th month on the Jewish calendar is the Jewish New Year, Rosh Hashanah: the Feast of Trumpets. It was time for a fresh start, a new life, a repentance that brought restoration. What did Ezra do?

Who was his audience? Why?

The service lasted six hours! What does verse 3 say about the receptiveness of the people?

Record Matthew 5:6.

Personal: Does this describe the state of your heart toward the Lord? If not, go back and read Revelation 2:5 with a prayerful heart asking the Lord to increase your hunger!

5. Ezra taught as one anointed. He stood upon a wooden pulpit raised high above the people with 13 others who helped him read out loud (very loud). What promise is found in Jeremiah 29:13 to all who seek the Lord whole-heartedly?

Over the next few days we will be given six important steps to personal revival through our study of Nehemiah. Re-read Nehemiah 8 and see how many you can discover on your own.

1.
2.
3.
4.
5.
6.

6. Continue to work on your memory verse for this week. How much can you record without looking?

DAY 4 – BEGIN IN PRAYER

1. Read Nehemiah 8.

2. Today we will discover the first three of six steps to personal revival. The first one is found at the end of verse 5, what did the action of the people reveal about their attitude toward the Word of God?

How does Luke 4:14-20 give us an example of the high priority placed upon the written Word of God?

3. The first step to bringing about personal revival in your life is cultivating a reverence for God's Word. How do the following Scriptures reveal the importance of God's Word in the life of the believer?

a. Job 23:12

b. Psalm 19:7-11

c. Jeremiah 15:16

d. Psalm 119:72

e. Psalm 119:97

Extra Credit Blessings!

f. Psalm 119:103, 104

g. Psalm 119:111

4. The second step to bringing about personal revival in your life is found in Nehemiah 8:6. What is it?

What call to worship is given to us in Psalm 95:6-7?

How would having a more worshipful approach to God change our outlook on our lives, and the circumstances and hardships in them?

Read and meditate on the call to worship found in Psalm 96:1-9. Selah!

5. Read Nehemiah 8:7, 8. What is the third step we must take in order to bring about personal revival in our lives?

Ezra and the men with him made the important decision to teach the people God's Word. They read distinctly from the book, in the Law of God, giving sense and understanding to the reading. This third step to personal revival is found in the diligent, committed, personal study of God's Word, individually and corporately within the church. What invaluable truth is found in Romans 10:17?

6. Continue to work on your memory verse for this week. How much can you record without looking?

DAY 5 – BEGIN IN PRAYER

1. Read Nehemiah 8.

2. Ezra and the teachers of Israel began to teach the people. They read distinctly, giving sense and understanding to the reading. The real key for study is reading and expositional teaching of the Word. List the first three of six steps to personal revival:
   1.
   2.
   3.

3. The reading and teaching of the Word of God brought understanding to the people and the result was deep conviction as the people applied the Word to their lives. Unfortunately, too often, we listen to gain information, or to analyze presentation, or to find fault and disagree. This type of hearing doesn't produce sanctification in our lives. First, we must have a deep reverence for the Word, and then approach the Lord with a heart of worship. When the people heard the reading of the Word and the teaching, what occurred in their lives? (v. 9)

It is not enough for us to know about God's Word or even understand His requirements for our lives. When we hear – we must respond in faith and obedience. What does James 1:22 say about hearing without a true heart response?

When the children of Israel heard the promises of God, they realized they had wasted many years and the sins of their forefathers had caused them much loss. This realization caused them to weep! What does Paul tell us about this godly sorrow in 2Corinthians 7:9-11?

The fourth step to personal revival is that after hearing God's Word we must personally apply it to our lives. What truth do we learn from Hebrews 4:12 about the power of the Word to penetrate a person's heart and bring about great change in a life submitted to the Lord Jesus Christ?

4. God's desire is to forgive our sins! Weeping is natural as we see our failures, but God through His Word leads us to hope in His restoration. We can receive forgiveness from the Lord by faith and move on in joy! The fifth step to personal revival is that when faith leads us to repentance then we must trust the Lord for true forgiveness, which in turn produces abundant joy! What promises do you find in the following Scriptures and how will you apply them to your life today?

   a. 1Peter 1:8

   b. John 15:11

   c. Galatians 5:22

5. On the first day the people met for a general assembly meeting and on the second day the rulers and leaders gathered to establish policies and practices based on the Scriptures. According to Nehemiah 8:14, 15, what were the people to do during the feast of the seventh month?

Read Leviticus 23:34-44. What was the name of this feast of the seventh month and why were the people to celebrate it every year?

When it was found written in the Law that the people were to celebrate the Feast of the Tabernacles, what did they do immediately?

The children of Israel were not content to just know what God said. They chose to obey it! The sixth step to personal revival is found in the example of the children of Israel, it's plain and simple: they obeyed! What do we learn about the importance of obedience from the following Scriptures?

   a. 1Samuel 15:22

   b. John 15:14

   c. 1John 5:3

6. Continue to work on your memory verse for this week. How much can you record without looking?

DAY 6 – BEGIN IN PRAYER

1. Read Nehemiah 7-8.

2. What lesson(s) from Nehemiah's life can you apply to your walk this week?

3. Record the six steps to personal revival.

    1.
    2.
    3.
    4.
    5.
    6.

Personal: Will you spend some time in prayer asking the Lord to make any needed changes in your heart so that you will find yourself with a fresh love, fresh fire, and fresh vision for your life!

4. Record your memory verse and the reference without looking! (It's important!)

DAY 1 – BEGIN IN PRAYER

1. Read Nehemiah 9.

2. The Feast of the Tabernacles was celebrated in Jerusalem for the first time since the days of Joshua. At the conclusion of the feast the nation gathers to pray in national commitment to God. It is one of the longest prayers recorded in the Bible. What is the spiritual attitude of the people?

What fresh commitment do they make?

3. What lesson(s) can you learn from this first reading of Nehemiah 9 that you will be able to apply in your walk with the Lord today?

DAY 2 – BEGIN IN PRAYER

1. Read Nehemiah 9.

2. It is interesting, and important to keep in mind, how many recorded prayers have the same pattern of recounting what God had done in the past for those who were praying. Read the following recorded prayers with this fact in mind.

   a. 1Kings 8:22-53

   b 2Samuel 7:18-29

   c. Acts 4:24-30

The purpose of the recounting was not to remind God, but rather it was to remind those in prayer of His goodness and His faithfulness. How does the Psalmist prompt us to recall the Lord's faithfulness in our lives?

   a. Psalm 103:2

   b. Psalm 105:5

3. Renewed in their resolve to follow the Lord, the people now come to seek God nationally. Israel was still in difficult straits; they were in the land, but they were without much power. Therefore, they turned to Him whose power is unsurpassed. According to Nehemiah 9:1-2, what action did the people take to illustrate the repentance in their hearts?

According to 2Corinthians 6:17, 18, what similar calling do we have on our lives when it comes to making a whole-hearted commitment to the Lord?

4. Like dry sponges soaking up water, these worshippers could not seem to get enough. How long did they stay before the Lord in worship and fellowship on this day after the Feast of Tabernacles? (v. 3)

I'm not sure how many of us would be ecstatic if the Sunday morning service at our church began to last six hours! Sadly, there is always a danger that anything routinely done will become a habit without heart! What can we do that will keep us from falling into the "habit of routine worship?"

How do the following Scriptures support your answer?

a. Ephesians 6:13-18

b. 1Thessalonians 5:17

c. 1Peter 1:13-19

5. The prayers of the people in Jerusalem began by acknowledging God. How would following their example affect the attitude with which we pray?

How does Matthew 6:9 illustrate this valuable truth?

What does Nehemiah 9:6 reveal about the One to Whom we have intimate access in prayer?

Personal: What do you need to take before His throne today? Will you? See Hebrews 4:16!

6. Choose a verse from today's lesson and begin today to commit it to memory!

DAY 3 – BEGIN IN PRAYER

1. Read Nehemiah 9.

2. In this prayer of the people, they declared that God had chosen them according to His will by choosing Abram (High Father), calling him out and giving him a new name, Abraham (Father of many nations). As God has chosen Abraham, so He has chosen you, a believer in Jesus Christ. What does 1Peter 2:9 teach you about who you are in Christ?

What else do we learn about our identity in Christ?

   a. Ephesians 1:4, 5

   b. Ephesians 5:8

   c. Titus 2:14

   d. 1John 3:1

3. The LORD had found Abraham faithful even though he had plenty of flaws. His faith in God covered his transgressions and weaknesses. God had made a covenant with him regarding the Promised Land and He would keep His Word! We can count on His Word! What promises are given to us regarding God's Word?

   a. Isaiah 55:11

   b. Matthew 24:35

c. 1Peter 1:23-25

4. In their prayer the people remembered the faithfulness of God to His Word and reminded themselves that when He saw the affliction of their fathers in Egypt, He heard their cry by the Red Sea. In God's timing, deliverance came to His people. As God worked, He developed a reputation in the world as God Almighty, the Lord God of Israel. One day all people of the earth will praise Jesus. Use Philippians 2:9-11 as a reminder that our victory is certain! How does this improve your outlook on today?

5. What direction are we given in Matthew 5:16 and what will be the outcome of our obedience to this command?

God had made a name for Himself through His dealings with Israel. Today He chooses to use the church to bring Him glory. He had delivered Israel from their enemies; He led them day and night; He taught them His good Law and fed them, daily renewing His promises to them...and yet...how did they return the favor? What is the first word of Nehemiah 9:16?

6. Continue to work on your memory verse for this week. How much can you record without looking?

DAY 4 – BEGIN IN PRAYER

1. Read Nehemiah 9.

2. Beginning in Nehemiah 9:16, the prayer of praise turns into a prayer of confession. They declared that God was faithful and they confessed that they had not been. If there is ever distance between you and God, who moved?

Why do we know this to be true?

a. Deuteronomy 31:8

b. 1Samuel 12:22

c. Psalm 37:28a

d. Hebrews 13:5

3. In this prayer of the people we find an excellent example of true repentance. The people admitted it was they who had moved, rebelled and turned from His good Word! They had heard the Word of God without responding in obedience; they had walked away from the conviction that God was right and they desperately needed Him. They had forgotten His many miracles on their behalf and they had even made plans to return to Egypt. What counsel was given to the church of Ephesus in Revelation 2:4, 5 when they found themselves away from God's love?

In the midst of their defiance, the nature of God – His everlasting love – is clearly revealed. The God of the Old Testament is not a God of wrath, but a God of mercy, and He is the same yesterday, today, and forever. How did He reveal Himself to Moses in Exodus 34:5-8?

The magnificent news for us today is, that God is God, and He is ready to pardon. There is not a sin, or a multitude of sins that cannot be forgiven. What promise is made to you today in 1John 1:9?

4. The children of Israel were able to boldly declare, "In Your manifold mercies You did not forsake them in the wilderness." Record Psalm 130:3, 4.

Write a prayer of praise and thanksgiving to your Heavenly Father because His mercies endure forever.

5. Nehemiah 9:21 tells us that the people lacked nothing! The LORD provided for their every need through 40 years of wandering! Unfortunately, the people delighted themselves in God's goods, but not in His goodness; they lived in God's land, but would not follow God's law; they wanted God's blessings, but wanted nothing to do with God Himself. What warning did God give through Moses to the people before they entered the Promised Land in Deuteronomy 8:1-14?

What part of the warning and command of Deuteronomy 8 can you apply to your walk with Jesus today that will strengthen your relationship and help you to align your priorities?

6. Continue to work on your memory verse for this week. How much can you record without looking?

DAY 5 – BEGIN IN PRAYER

1. Read Nehemiah 9.

2. During the days of the Judges, the cycle of sin was repeated six times. The sad details are recorded in the Book of Judges. The people would turn their backs on the True, and Living God, He would send judgment in the form of an enemy nation, they would repent, and then God would send a deliverer. What tragic statement is made in Judges 21:25?

3. Despite God's constant mercy and goodness, the people were slow to learn! What was God's heart toward His people according to Nehemiah 9:31?

What is His heart like toward you, as His son or daughter?

   a. John 3:16, 17

   b. Romans 5:8, 9

c. 1Peter 3:18

d. 1John 4:9, 10

4. As the confession of the people continued, notice that they took full responsibility for the hardship and punishment in their lives. They did not blame God! What do they state about the character of God in Nehemiah 9:33?

What warning and encouragement is given to us in Galatians 6:7-9?

5. Finally, beginning in verse 32, we read the petition, or request, of their prayer. What was it that the people had learned about God and His dealings with them?

What was their request?

It is vitally important that we, as believers, learn these important foundational truths: God is Good; God is Just; God is righteous; and God is Love! Find four verses that teach us these truths.

1.

2.

3.

4.

If you really believe this to be true, it will keep you from asking the question, "If God is so just, why does He allow..." Record the foundational truth of Romans 8:28.

6. Continue to work on your memory verse for this week. How much can you record without looking?

DAY 6 – BEGIN IN PRAYER

1. Read Nehemiah 9.

2. What lesson(s) from Nehemiah's life can you apply to your walk this week?

3. Israel found themselves as a nation on their knees in this awesome day of national repentance. Loudly proclaiming their guilt and God's goodness; they came to make a new covenant of promise with Him; to put it in writing, to start over, to begin again to live His way! What invitation is extended to us in Isaiah 55:6-9?

Personal: If you have found room for repentance in your walk with the Lord this week, will you write a new covenant of promise to the Lord Jesus Christ, committing every area of your life to His use and for His service?

4. Record your memory verse and the reference without looking! (It's important!)

DAY 1 – BEGIN IN PRAYER

1. Read Nehemiah 10.

2. The book of Nehemiah covers a historic time in Israel's past; it was a time of great revival for which we get a front row seat and an excellent peek at the activity behind the scenes. We are able to study the prayer of a nation who jointly admitted their sin of turning away from God, coming to Him in repentance, begging for forgiveness and restoration. Many folks start off to serve the Lord whole-heartedly, but sadly end up where Israel had been for years, far from Him. What happened in their spiritual walk that caused this to occur?

The lesson of chapter 10 is about setting Biblical goals, or perhaps we could say, putting first things first! According to Mark 12:30, what is to be the number one goal in your life, your first priority, above and beyond everything else?

3. What lesson(s) can you learn from this first reading of Nehemiah 10 that you will be able to apply in your walk with the Lord today?

DAY 2 – BEGIN IN PRAYER

1. Read Nehemiah 10.

2. It is easy in daily life to let the urgent replace the vital. Even when all the urgent fires are out a more stubborn fire continues to burn – the one started by our neglect of the important daily commitment to the Lord! Like the children of Israel, we must prioritize our life practices and pursue actions that will begin to undo the effects of sin and neglect upon our relationship with God. Revival must lead to action! What must you do <u>daily</u>, as a Christian, to ensure a healthy, vital relationship with the Lord?

How will heeding the following Scriptures strengthen and protect your faith?

a. John 4:23, 24

b. 1Thessalonians 5:17

c. 2Timothy 2:15

d. James 1:22

3. As we have learned from studying Nehemiah's life, goal setting is biblical and extremely important in the life of every believer. We cannot excuse our lack of diligence, planning, or commitment by using the cop out, "God will work it out!" It is true, He will, but we are to do our best work so that He will receive all honor and glory. How does Colossians 3:23, 24 speak to this truth?

Personal: Think back to the time you first committed your life to Jesus Christ, the time you acknowledged to Him your need for a Savior, and surrendered your life to Him. Is your current commitment to Jesus stronger or weaker? Are there any changes that must be made?

(If you haven't yet asked Jesus to forgive your sins or trusted Him for forgiveness and salvation, the Bible says, today is the day of salvation – Ask Him, He is waiting – See Revelation 3:20 and John 3:16).

4. These men and women in Jerusalem made a covenant with the Lord, they committed themselves to making core value changes. These were hard choices that would cost them, but they determined their relationship with the Lord must come first regardless of the cost. What type of devotion is required from the follower of Jesus Christ?

In Luke 14:25-35, what challenge is given by our Lord Jesus to those who would be His disciples?

What warning is given in the following Scriptures to those who try to serve the Lord and the world?

a. Luke 9:62

b. Luke 16:13

c. Revelation 3:16

5. This matter of total commitment is not to be taken lightly, what choice did Joshua set before the people of Israel in Joshua 24:15?

How did they respond according to Joshua 24:16, 17?

6. Choose a verse from today's lesson and begin today to commit it to memory!

DAY 3 – BEGIN IN PRAYER

1. Read Nehemiah 10.

2. The people set Biblical goals, they made new or fresh commitments to the Lord, and they sealed it with their signature. As a follower of the Lord Jesus Christ, we have made a choice to surrender our life, heart, and will to Him. How does Paul describe himself in light of his surrender to Jesus Christ in Romans 1:1?

Use a Dictionary of Bible Words to define the word bondservant from Romans 1:1.

3. How does a bondservant live?

   a. Matthew 5:16

   b. Luke 9:23

   c. 1Corinthians 6:19, 20

d. 1Peter 2:9-12

e. Romans 6:11-14

4. Eighty-four names are listed in Nehemiah 10:1-27, and verse 28 adds all those not mentioned by name who where old enough to comprehend God's commands. God requires a choice by each individual. The eternal question asked by Jesus to his disciples in Matthew 16:15 must be addressed. What is it?

Personal: Who do you say that He is?

Since we know that each individual is required to make a choice to follow Him, what Scriptures would you use to share this truth with someone who has not yet trusted Jesus as his or her Lord and Savior?

5. Even as believers, there are times, like with these Israelites, that a recommitment is necessary. Sadly, too easily, and too often, the stuff of the flesh and the world contaminate our walk with the Lord. What act did Jesus perform in John 13:5-15?

What was the lesson and how can you specifically apply it to your life today?

6. Continue to work on your memory verse for this week. How much can you record without looking?

DAY 4 – BEGIN IN PRAYER

1. Read Nehemiah 10.

2. With this new commitment established and the hearts of the people ignited toward obedience, they were now faced with the challenge of cleansing their personal and national lives of practices that were opposed to the

commandments, ordinances, and statutes of the LORD. According to verses 30 and 31, what changes did they need to make?

Take note of the unity that was at work here amongst the people, these joined with their brethren, their nobles, and entered into a curse and an oath to walk in God's Law...They decided the best way to stay on track in their lives was to do it together. This teamwork provided both accountability and encouragement. How does Ecclesiastes 4:9-12 describe the value of this joint effort?

3. What do we learn about the necessity of being an active part of a group of believers who desire God's best for their lives?

   a. Romans 15:1, 2

   b. Galatians 6:1, 2

   c. 1Thessalonians 5:14

   d. Hebrews 10:25

4. According to verse 30, what decision was made regarding their relationship with the unbelievers amongst them?

Upon entering the Promised Land, what steps were the Israelites to take against the inhabitants of Canaan according to Deuteronomy 7:1-3?

Why was such a drastic action required? (Deuteronomy 7:4-6)

Note: This seemingly harsh judgment is truly a picture of the LORD's grace and mercy. God had waited over 400 years to bring judgment on a group of nations whose lifestyle and pagan worship was repulsive and contemptible to Him. See Genesis 15:12-16.

Idolaters surrounded the nation of Israel and they could have easily lost their identity by conforming to the world rather than following God's commands for their lives. Since they had fallen before in this area, they now vow to put a stop to this practice of intermarrying. In like manner, according to 2Corinthians 6:14-18, what instruction is given to the church regarding our relationship to the world?

5. From Nehemiah 10:31, what other covenants did the people vow to faithfully obey?

God had made a covenant with Israel back in Exodus. What do we learn about the purpose of the Sabbath from Exodus 31:13-18?

The observation of the Sabbath was meant to establish a day of rest for the people, a day that was to be devoted to seeking and worshipping God. What had happened that caused the people to neglect the Sabbath, and why do you think it happened?

The Sabbath was also to be a type of the rest Jesus would give to every person who stopped seeking to work his or her way into God's presence and trusted in His finished work on the cross at Calvary. How does Hebrews 4:1-11 describe this Sabbath rest that is ours in Jesus Christ?

At the end of Nehemiah 10:31 the people also contracted to forego the seventh year's produce and the exacting of every debt. The Sabbath Law was also to be applied to the land itself. According to Leviticus 25 on the seventh year the people were to refrain from planting any crops in order to give the soil a year of rest – but it never happened! This disobedience was partially the cause of the 70 years of captivity in Babylon. (2Chronicles 36:21) What lesson would the people have learned by obeying this command of God?

In the end, the disobedience cost the people far more than they would have ever imagined, and it will be the same for us when we choose not to put the Lord and His ways first in our lives. In the nuts and bolts of living, God will honor the person who honors Him. What does John 12:25, 26 teach us about what should be our highest priority in life?

6. Continue to work on your memory verse for this week. How much can you record without looking?

DAY 5 – BEGIN IN PRAYER

1. Read Nehemiah 10.

2. The phrase the house of God (our LORD) is used nine times in Nehemiah 10:32-39. According to the law of God the people were always required to bring the firstfruits of all their increase (10%: the tithe). In spite of heavy taxation and poverty, they commit to first things first! What ordinance did the people establish according to Nehemiah 10:32-33?

Along with this self-imposed tax to subsidize the costs of the daily sacrifices that were prescribed by God for their national life, what other services did the people provide as they sought to obey God in their daily practice of worship?

It is clear that the work and service of corporate worship required a consistent group effort. No one could accomplish the work on his or her own. Use a Bible Dictionary to define and learn more about the meaning of firstfruits as spoken of in verses 35-39.

3. What do we learn about the firstfruits from the following Scriptures?

    a. Exodus 22:29, 30

    b. Exodus 23:19

    c. Proverbs 3:9, 10

Note: Of course firstlings from the children could not be sacrificed, but rather they were redeemed in kind, as were the cattle!

4. The issue, therefore, is about our willingness to give. This is a very difficult area of our lives to fully surrender to the Lord. The bottom line truth is, all that we have comes from Him and all He asks for is a tenth back. This giving back

acknowledges and recognizes that the source of all our blessings come from Him. What do we learn from James 1:17 regarding every blessing in our lives?

A willingness to give is solely the work of God in the heart of each believer, and it is the only method through which the needs of the church, as a whole, are satisfied. Giving habits do reflect the condition of the heart. What does Matthew 10:8b teach us about how we ought to give?

What wisdom is found in the words of King Solomon in Ecclesiastes 5:13?

It seems that the Law of the Firstfruits is a real offense to our flesh (particularly in our society). Yet, as we surrender our lives to the Lord, as these Israelites with Nehemiah had chosen to do, our priorities will move us to let go and obey God's command to give. What instructions and promises about giving do we find in 2Corinthians 9:6-9?

5. What more do we learn about the sacrifice of giving from the following Scriptures?

   a. Deuteronomy 16:17

   b. Proverbs 11:24, 25

   c. Acts 20:35

   d. Galatians 6:7-10

Attached to giving is God's promise to bless in return, yet this is not to be the motive for our giving. What strong words of rebuke, with promise, are given to us through the Prophet Malachi in Malachi 3:6-12?

Personal: Is there room for improvement in your giving, whether it is time, talents, or financial support of your local body? If you are not willing to let go, perhaps it is because you have forgotten that it is not yours to begin with (1Timothy 6:17-19).

6. Continue to work on your memory verse for this week. How much can you record without looking?

DAY 6 – BEGIN IN PRAYER

1. Read Nehemiah 10.

2. What lesson(s) from Nehemiah's life can you apply to your walk this week?

3. The vows of the people in Jerusalem were made: they were willing to return to God's way, while forsaking self-interest, they committed to becoming and remaining separate from the unbelievers around them, and they began to obediently practice daily worship of the LORD through giving and serving. What we see in their lives is priority in action! What exhortation are you given in Matthew 6:33? How will obeying this command affect your walk this week?

4. Record your memory verse and the reference without looking! (It's important!)

DAY 1 – BEGIN IN PRAYER

1. Read Nehemiah 11.

2. Having taken the steps to recommit to the LORD, both personally and nationally, revival captured the hearts of the people. God gives us the on-going story of the work of the Holy Spirit in the restoration of the city and its people. What do you see by this first reading of chapter 11 that reveals God's plans and direction in the people's lives?

3. What lesson(s) can you learn from this first reading of Nehemiah 11 that you will be able to apply in your walk with the Lord today?

DAY 2 – BEGIN IN PRAYER

1. Read Nehemiah 11.

2. When Zerrubabel and Joshua left Babylon to return to Jerusalem in 536BC (91 years earlier) they had about 50,000 people with them. Only a couple thousand more had come with Ezra in 457BC and fewer still with Nehemiah in 445BC. By the grace of God the walls were up and in place, but the work was far from complete. Imagine what the daily living conditions might have been like in Jerusalem at this time and write a brief description.

Chapter 11 is a chapter of unsung heroes! It is the who's who of those that no one knows, except the LORD Himself! The details that are revealed to us in this chapter are the natural fruit and outgrowth of the heart commitment made in the last chapter. The outgrowth of relationship is service. One of the main lessons we will learn this week is that service for the Lord is of utmost value regardless of whether it is seen or unseen! Read 1Corinthians 12:12-27 – how does the truth of these verses apply to the situation in Jerusalem in Nehemiah's day?

How can you apply it to your service in the church today?

3. By moving into the city, the rulers themselves set the pace as they sought to lead the people by their example of self-sacrifice and trust in the Lord. It

is of absolute importance that leaders lead by example. What invitation and exhortation did the Apostle Paul extend to those who served the Lord with Him?

a. 1Corinthians 4:15, 16

b. 1Corinthians 11:1

c. 2Thessalonians 3:7-9

According to 1Peter 5:1-5, how are spiritual leaders to lead and how are they to serve?

4. Following the example of the leaders, the people agreed together to cast lots and thereby determine the will of God for each family. One out of ten would move into town. It was a commitment of faith for everyone. What does Nehemiah 11:2 teach us about the attitude of those who volunteered to dwell in Jerusalem?

These volunteers were moved by the Holy Spirit and willing to accept the hardship of living in a desolate place. They willingly offered, literally they were incited from within, to take this bold step of faith. They pulled up roots, left the comforts that they may have established, and made their service to God and His plans the chief impetus of their lives. Revisit the exhortation in Matthew 6:33 that we studied at the end of last week. How does it describe the actions and attitudes of these faithful servants in Jerusalem?

5. What more do we learn about the heart of willing sacrifice and commitment that is an essential character trait of the believer?

a. Matthew 5:6

b. Matthew 6:19-21

c. John 6:27

d. Romans 14:16-19

e. Colossians 3:1-3

6. Choose a verse from today's lesson and begin today to commit it to memory!

DAY 3 – BEGIN IN PRAYER

1. Read Nehemiah 11.

2. Nehemiah 11:3-24, lists names and various groups who came to stay in Jerusalem. The majority were descendants of Judah and Benjamin, who had been given the area in and around Jerusalem when the land was divided amongst the twelve tribes. The number of those from the tribes of Judah and Benjamin was 1396. The priests and their families numbered 1192. The priests were to dwell in the midst of the city to be the spiritual leaders to encourage and strengthen the people. As a part of the Body of Christ, we can learn much from their example. What have we learned so far about each of the following aspects of Body Ministry?

    a. The value of each part in its contribution to the whole:

    b. The right motivation to serve:

    c. The importance of leadership example:

    d. The need for teamwork and support in the church:

3. This list of who's who, or those who most people don't know, includes faithful people from every walk of life, with many different gifts and talents. How is the church described in Romans 12:4, 5?

How are we to serve one another, according to Romans 12:6-9?

4. Finding our part in the work of the Lord can be difficult, especially when the flesh, which longs to be seen and honored, recognized and acknowledged, can sometimes complicate it. Any call of God to a place of service that is behind the scene may be met with resistance from our old nature. According to Matthew 16:24, 25, what is the cure for this battle?

How do you think faithfully serving in the following manner would change the direction of the church?

a. Matthew 19:29

b. Mark 8:35

c. Luke 9:23-26

d. John 12:25, 26

e. Acts 20:24

Personal: How would faithfully serving in the above manner change the direction of your life?

5. The flesh needs to be overcome at all costs! What instruction does Paul give us in Ephesians 6:5-8 regarding how we are to serve?

6. Continue to work on your memory verse for this week. How much can you record without looking?

DAY 4 – BEGIN IN PRAYER

1. Read Matthew 20:20-28.

2. Jesus warned us of the importance of serving with the right heart and with the correct motive. What was that warning from Matthew 6:1-4?

3. Record the main details of the incident that took place in Matthew 20:20-28.

4. Perhaps James and John put their mom up to the task of approaching Jesus with this request. How does the Lord respond to the request? Who does He speak to directly?

A prayer for glory is really a request to suffer. The question posed to these two brothers was, "can you drink the cup?" Read the following account of another encounter involving the "sons of Zebedee" and Jesus from Matthew 26:36-46. What was the occasion?

What is referred to by the phrase "this cup"?

How did these brothers respond?

It is clear that it is pride that incites us to boast in our own ability. What does Proverbs 16:18 teach us about pride?

What other warnings about the sin of pride are found in the following Proverbs?

a. Proverbs 8:13

b. Proverbs 14:3

c. Proverbs 29:23

5. James and John would suffer much for Jesus' name. John would eventually be arrested and placed in boiling oil, but spared by God and exiled to Patmos

in his old age. According to Acts 12:1, 2 what happened to James when the persecution began in Jerusalem?

According to Matthew 20:24, what was the response of the other 10 disciples? Why do you think they reacted in this manner?

6. Continue to work on your memory verse for this week. How much can you record without looking?

DAY 5 – BEGIN IN PRAYER

1. Read Matthew 20:20-28.

2. The Lord used this encounter with James, John, and their mother to teach the difference between the world and being a member of the Body of Christ. The world places great stock in position and power, the church is to be just the opposite, placing its greatest value on the lifestyle of a lowly servant. What had started as a play for stardom by two Apostles, ended as a lesson in servanthood for those who really wanted to see Jesus honored and no one else. What is the difference between worldly leadership and the leadership in the church?

Why did the Son of Man come?

How then are we to serve according to Philippians 2:1-8?

What instructions are added in the following Scriptures regarding the lifestyle of the servant of the Lord?

a. Romans 12:10-21

b. Ephesians 4:1-3

Personal: How would you rate your servanthood walk in light of the above Scriptures? What needs to be changed – today?

3. Back to Nehemiah. Revival had brought the people joy in the Lord, and a willingness to serve Him despite the cost, or the outward reward that might follow. A good indicator of the moving of the Holy Spirit is seen when the body, in response to being asked "why" they are involved somewhere, is able to answer, "the Lord has put us here!" What does 1Corinthians 12:4-11 say about spiritual gifts and the Giver of gifts?

4. As members of the Body of Christ, the requirement for us is daily surrender and faithful obedience, no matter where we have been assigned to serve. Jesus instructed His disciples about the necessity of humility in the life of His children. What do we learn from Luke 14:8-11 regarding humility and exaltation?

5. Most of the ministries in the church are unseen, from the nursery to the prison ministry, from the janitor to those working in the office, from the mission trip to the helps ministry, few are ever seen or honored – but God keeps great records as Nehemiah 11 clearly teaches us! Let's revisit 1Corinthians 12:19-27, what insight into the importance of body ministry have you gained today?

Again the question is how can you apply it to your service in the church today?

As in our physical body, so in our spiritual one, the most vital parts (organs) are unseen. You can live without an eye or ear, finger or toe, but not without your lungs, or your heart, or your brain. God is ready to bless any unsung potential hero whose only concern is serving the Lord and not for getting the glory. These faithful men and women in Jerusalem had experienced spiritual revival, they recommitted themselves to obeying the Word of God, and they were filled with joy, serving in anonymity for love was compelling them. As we follow their example, what will be said of our witness?

a. 1Thessalonians 1:2, 3

b. 1Thessalonians 1:7, 8

c. 2Thessalonians 1:3-4

6. Continue to work on your memory verse for this week. How much can you record without looking?

DAY 6 – BEGIN IN PRAYER

1. Read Nehemiah 11.

2. What lesson(s) from Nehemiah's life can you apply to your walk this week?

3. Do you know any unsung heroes in the faith? Spend a moment thanking the Lord for them and making mention of them in your prayers!

God's gifts and calling make you invaluable to the body and the work of God. According to 1Corinthians 4:2, what is required of you?

What does Ephesians 4:7 say that gives you the assurance of acceptance?

4. Record your memory verse and the reference without looking! (It's important!)

DAY 1 – BEGIN IN PRAYER

1. Read Nehemiah 12.

2. The completed wall was celebrated with great joy. Along with a detailed list of the priests and the Levites, what act of praise takes place in chapter 12?

What did the people have to worship about?

How is it that they were able to worship in light of the fact that they were still facing great hardship and danger? How can you? Do you?

3. What lesson(s) can you learn from this first reading of Nehemiah 12 that you will be able to apply in your walk with the Lord today?

DAY 2 – BEGIN IN PRAYER

1. Read Nehemiah 12.

2. If joy were a disease, it would be listed as extremely contagious. People with real joy in life are always in demand; we love hanging around joyful people: but they are a rare find in the midst of the grumbling downcast masses…and we're talking about church people. Yet, the Lord has promised His children "fullness of joy" and we see it here with Nehemiah in Jerusalem – there was joy on the wall! According to Nehemiah, who were the leaders of this worship celebration?

How did Nehemiah position the choirs?

Nehemiah led one group of worshippers, who did he send with the other?

The list of priests and scribes in chapter 12 covers several generations, the fathers who had returned with Zerrubabel and Joshua about 90 years earlier and their sons who assumed the family leadership position in this current generation. What prominent names do you see among the list?

3. The purpose of this dedication worship service was to acknowledge, and remind the people, that it had been the LORD who had allowed them, and equipped them to build this wall. What do we learn about our own ability to serve and accomplish God's work from John 15:5?

It is absolutely true that without Him we can do nothing, however, the tremendous good news is, if we abide in Him, we will bear much fruit. The people in Jerusalem were not gifted wall builders, but they were willing servants who fully trusted God to use them. Therefore, what can you do for Jesus as you abide in Him?

a. Philippians 4:13

b. John 15:17

c. 2Corinthians 3:2-5

What additional truths are we given through the following Scriptures that remind us that we are simply a vessel of HIS work?

a. James 1:17

b. 2Peter 1:2-4

4. The worship service was to be a time of gladness, thanksgiving, singing, music, and much more. For the dedication they sought out, amongst the Levites in the neighboring communities, musicians, worship leaders, and priests. The act of worship is to be an act of celebration! Music and song are

elements of worship, but much more is required. Read this early account of worship in Genesis 22:1-14 – what was the context of Abraham's worship?

Sometimes, it is too easy for us to go through the motions without engaging our hearts. What reminders do we find from the following Scriptures about the motive, the attitude, and the action of worship?

a. 1Chronicles 16:29-34

b. Psalm 95:1-6

c. John 4:23, 24

5. Before the festivities what action had to be taken by the priests and the people according to Nehemiah 12:30?

Holiness must precede joy! What must occur in the heart of the believer in order to be prepared for true worship?

6. Choose a verse from today's lesson and begin today to commit it to memory!

Day 3 – Begin in Prayer

1. Read Nehemiah 12.

2. According to Nehemiah 12:31, who led this worship team?

Nehemiah and the leaders of Judah ascended the city walls and the tribes circled the city. One group went east with Ezra, the other west led by Nehemiah. What an awesome scene it must have been – an entire city worshipping the LORD! How did Nehemiah describe this worship in 12:43?

Why were they rejoicing?

With what modern day event could you compare the sound and excitement of this worship celebration in Jerusalem?

3. How does the Psalmist describe and encourage us in our worship of the Lord?

   a. Psalm 27:6

   b. Psalm 28:7

   c. Psalm 30:11, 12

   d. Psalm 81:1, 2

   e. Psalm 98:4-6

Personal: How does this enthusiastic worship compare with yours?

4. Nehemiah 12:43 says, they offered great sacrifices, and rejoiced, for God had made them rejoice with great joy…This joy was not an emotion that they could produce within themselves, it was a by product of their new commitment to the LORD. It was the outcome of their relationship. What does Psalm 16:11 teach about the source of joy?

The people expressed their joy in singing, in serving, in giving, and in the commitments they had made. True joy comes from doing as God has instructed. Joy is the fruit of obedience. According to 1John 4:19, why do we love Jesus?

5. Use the following Scriptures as a reminder to your heart of the finished work that the Lord has accomplished in your life.

   a. 1John 4:10

b. Ephesians 2:4, 5

c. Titus 3:3-5

6. Continue to work on your memory verse for this week. How much can you record without looking?

DAY 4 – BEGIN IN PRAYER

1. Read John 15.

2. Nehemiah and the people of Jerusalem were filled with joy that spilled over, and was displayed in their words and their deeds. Joy in the Lord is God's will for every believer! It is God's will for you! The joy of the Lord is spoken of often in the New Testament. What does John 15:9-11 teach us about this joy?

Sadly, many Christians seem to lack fullness of joy, living to a certain extent under a constant cloud of disappointment. Paul told the Ephesians that a Spirit-filled life would produce joyfulness of heart. What do we learn from Ephesians 5:18-20 and how will you put it into practice in your life today?

3. The Greek word for joy is chara and it is used some seventy times in the New Testament. By definition this joy always refers to a state of heart, which is based on believing spiritual realities. It is the result of an internal perspective; it is the spiritual choice of making God's outlook our own! What instruction is given in the following Scriptures that is imperative to follow and believe, if we are going to walk in fullness of joy?

   a. John 15:9-12

   b. John 16:23, 24

c. 1Thessalonians 5:16

d. 1John 1:1-4

4. This joy and peace that comes from believing and trusting the God of hope stands in direct contrast to the joy found in the world, which is defined as an emotional feeling dependent on favorable outward circumstances; as a result this worldly joy is fleeting and superficial, and empty. Yet heavenly joy is a spiritual condition, a fruit of relationship with Jesus and it cannot be affected by circumstances. What does Galatians 5:22, 23 teach us about heavenly joy?

What direction is added in Galatians 5:24-26?

5. How and why is it possible for the believer to have joy even through difficult circumstances and severe tragedies?

   a. John 17:12-16

   b. 1Peter 1:6-9

6. Continue to work on your memory verse for this week. How much can you record without looking?

DAY 5 – BEGIN IN PRAYER

1. Read John 16.

2. We continue today to study the issue of spiritual joy – the joy of the Lord. According to John 16:33, what promise are we given for victory?

Read Romans 14:17-19, what is the kingdom of God and what are we, as its citizens, to pursue?

What important lesson did we learn from Nehemiah 8:10-12?

3. Heavenly joy is an outlook of mind and heart that is aware of God's love, God's ways, and God's promises. It may or may not be emotional, but it is secure, and certain for God never changes. What declaration did the Psalmist make in Psalm 4:6-8?

Personal: How does your joy and rest compare to the Psalmist's?
Biblical, spiritual joy is always the by-product of knowing and following the Lord. What song of rejoicing filled Isaiah's heart according to Isaiah 61:10? Will you make it yours today?

4. It is God Himself who fills us with joy. How is this made clear through Paul's prayer for the Romans in Romans 15:13?

How can we not be overflowing with joy as we consider God and His love, God and His word, and all that He has done for us! Read Psalm 40 – record a verse that causes your heart to rejoice and meditate on it throughout the day!

5. When we allow the obstacles in our lives to become stumbling blocks to our faith in the Lord, we sacrifice our joy in Him. Find a Scripture for each of the following circumstances that, when heeded would keep you from sin, and therefore, keep you from losing your joy.

   If you're worried or afraid:

   If you're lonely or discouraged:

   If you're angry:

   If you're mistreated:

If you're tempted by evil:

If you're ____________:

6. Continue to work on your memory verse for this week. How much can you record without looking?

DAY 6 – BEGIN IN PRAYER

1. Read Nehemiah 12.

2. What lesson(s) from Nehemiah's life can you apply to your walk this week?

3. By studying the life of Nehemiah and those who recommitted their lives to the Lord in Jerusalem, how have you been challenged to examine your joy this week?

The secret to living a life filled with the joy of the Lord is really no secret at all! What must we do to fully experience the joy of the Lord?

What exhortation is given to the church in Philippians 4:4? Are you willing to choose to do so beginning now?

4. Record your memory verse and the reference without looking! (It's important!)

DAY 1 – BEGIN IN PRAYER

1. Read Nehemiah 13:1-14.

2. Nehemiah had come to Jerusalem in the 20th year of Artaxerxes. He was in Jerusalem for about twelve years serving as their governor, builder, and leader before returning to Persia in the 32nd year of the reign of Artaxerxes. What had happened in Jerusalem during Nehemiah's journey to Persia?

What was Nehemiah's response to this tragic turn of events?

What action did he take?

3. What lesson(s) can you learn from this first reading of Nehemiah 13:1-14 that you will be able to apply in your walk with the Lord today?

DAY 2 – BEGIN IN PRAYER

1. Read Nehemiah 13:1-14.

2. In Nehemiah 13:1-3 we find a transitional phrase that gives us the final words about the on-going revival and dedication of the people and their commitment to follow the word of the Lord. What instructions were found and what actions were taken?

3. Within just a few years we find the people completely retreating from their devotion and commitment becoming "lukewarm" or, even worse, having an openly defiant spiritual condition. The main lesson of chapter 13 is the importance of establishing a daily diligence in our walk with the Lord. We must stay alert, and press on, for even the most sincere saint can fall prey to the enemy, for he does not sleep. What does 1Peter 5:8 say about the enemy who seeks your destruction?

The Christian walk has been described as "an uphill skate" – if you stop moving forward, you will soon be rolling downhill! What safeguard does 1Peter 5:9 give us to withstand the continuous attack of the enemy?

4. The truth is, you can never rest when it comes to the care of your spiritual walk with the Lord! There is a battle on for your soul! What warnings are we given in the following verses, and how will you put them into practice in your life today?

    a. Mark 14:38

    b. Luke 21:34-36

    c. Romans 13:11-14

    d. Ephesians 6:17, 18

    e. 1Thessalonians 5:8

    f. 1Peter 4:7-10

5. From Nehemiah's life and his example of leadership we also learn that the task of discipleship, whether you are a pastor, parent, or friend, comes with built-in setbacks. The work of God is an on-going process that needs our constant diligence and strong leadership. We have been given the responsibility of caring for one another's lives within the church. What direction are we given in Hebrews 12:12-14 about this body ministry?

What added instruction are we given in Ephesians 4:29-32?

Personal: How closely does the above exhortation describe your life? Is there a particular area that needs added attention this week? Remember it is a closer walk that produces healthier fruit!

6. Choose a verse from today's lesson and begin today to commit it to memory!

DAY 3 – BEGIN IN PRAYER

1. Read Nehemiah 13:1-14.

2. Nehemiah tells us he had returned to see the king in Shushan and he must have stayed there for quite sometime for much had transpired while he was away. According to verses 4 and 5, what alliance had taken place in Jerusalem?

What move had they made regarding the usage of the storerooms in the Temple?

Who was this man Tobiah?

How might the truth of James 4:4 apply to this sinful alliance with Tobiah?

3. Nehemiah's description of the spiritual decline that took place in Jerusalem while he was away reveals the importance of daily discipline and constant diligence in our spiritual walks. What does 1Corinthians 15:33 teach us about choosing our alliances carefully?

How will the following Scriptures help you in choosing your friends?

a. Proverbs 13:20

b. Psalm 119:63

c. 2Corinthians 6:14-18

4. Eliashib, the high priest, was the spiritual leader of the people. However, he failed in this because his friendship with the world was too strong and it turned his head from the things of God! What warning is given to us in 1John 2:15-17?

What had Nehemiah declared regarding this man Tobiah according to Nehemiah 2:19, 20?

Eliashib had connected himself to Tobiah through marriage (Tobiah and his son had both married Jewish women) and the effect was that the enemy had a strong alliance inside the walls. Remember, Tobiah was an Ammonite and an avowed enemy of God and His people. He had been opposing the work of God in Jerusalem from the beginning. According to Nehemiah 13:5, where was he living?

What had previously been stored in the room that was given to Tobiah?

5. As a result of the compromising leadership of Eliashib, the storerooms that were dedicated to contain the precious things of God now housed this evil man in all his glory. In like manner, if we are not diligent and disciplined in our spiritual walk, the things of the world can crowd out the precious things of God. Record the strong exhortation of Galatians 6:7, 8.

Personal: Is there anything of the world being stored in your life that is crowding out the precious fellowship of the Lord? If so, are you willing to cleanse the temple – the Lord is waiting to do so now!

Tobiah was to have no heritage or right or memorial in Jerusalem and yet, when Nehemiah left the country it was the high priest, the senior pastor if you will, who invited him into fellowship. No one is immune from this temptation to sin. The constant threat to our daily spiritual growth is Satan's attempt to introduce these "Tobiahs" into our lives so the enemy can camp where God should be worshipped! Read Psalm 1 and record a few important points from the Psalm that encourage your heart and your walk today.

6. Continue to work on your memory verse for this week. How much can you record without looking?

DAY 4 – BEGIN IN PRAYER

1. Read Nehemiah 13:1-14.

2. Fortunately, God brought Nehemiah back to Jerusalem and he soon got wind of all that had been going on during his absence. Imagine what he must of felt as he returned to see the sin of the leaders in Jerusalem. How is his reaction described in Nehemiah 13:8a?

What immediate action did he take, according to verses 8 and 9?

What similar type of event is detailed in the following Scriptures?

   a. John 2:13-17

   b. Matthew 21:12-16

3. As a true spiritual leader, Nehemiah was angry and disappointed with the high priest and his actions. His heart was broken over the sin and he quickly moved to bring things back to order. His anger was not out of defense of himself, but in defense of the honor and glory of God. This is sometimes described as "righteous anger." What instruction does Ephesians 4:26 give us regarding the emotion of anger?

What do we learn about the anger that is "not righteous" and its place in the life of the Christian?

   a. Psalm 37:8

   b. Ecclesiastes 7:9

   c. Ephesians 4:31, 32

4. Protecting the people and the church from compromise might be one of the hardest tasks a pastor, leader, or overseer must undertake. But, it must be done! What exhortation is given to the Christian leader in 1Peter 5:1-4?

What does Hebrews 13:17 teach us about how we are to respond to the leadership the Lord has set over us?

5. Nehemiah was a godly man who was able to make tough decisions in the care of God's flock. He would not and could not overlook sin when it was revealed. Even though his actions may not have been popular, it should be noted that our alliances will determine our character and Nehemiah made friends with those who sought the Lord. He chose to place eternal things first – at all cost. According to the following Scriptures, how should we follow his example?

   a. Ephesians 5:11

   b. Romans 16:17, 18

   c. 2Thessalonians 3:6 & 14

Personal: Who have you chosen as friends? Do they have the character to confront sin, if necessary?

6. Continue to work on your memory verse for this week. How much can you record without looking?

DAY 5 – BEGIN IN PRAYER

1. Read Nehemiah 13:1-14.

2. Once Nehemiah had departed from Jerusalem, the leaders and the people began to neglect the spiritual disciplines required by the LORD for worship. They quit giving to support the priests in the work of the Temple. With the High Priest being corrupted by the bad influences of compromise with the

world, what excuse would the people have, that is still prevalent today, for refusing to participate in worship?

How does 1Samuel 2:12-17 describe the priesthood in the days prior to the young prophet Samuel's ministry?

3. When a nation neglects, or rejects, its spiritual pursuits, it is immediately in grave danger of falling to so many other sins. It hadn't been that long since the people made the promise recorded in Nehemiah 10:35-39. What was their promise?

Why did they find themselves so far from the promise?

Personal: Are you closer or further away from the Lord than you were last year, last month, last week?

4. The backsliding of faith does not occur in one day – it results from the gradual neglect of that which brought and sustains our spiritual life. What strong reproof was the church of Ephesus given in Revelation 2:4, 5?

How will following Paul's example of Philippians 3:13, 14 keep you from falling or faltering in your faith?

What exhortation does 1Peter 1:13-16 give us than when heeded will protect us from neglecting our spiritual health?

How are you encouraged to diligence through the following Scriptures?

a. Hebrews 6:11, 12

b. Galatians 6:7-9

5. Looking back to Nehemiah in Jerusalem, he was not yet finished with clean up and restoration. There was much more to be done to restore the purity of the Temple. What question did he ask of the rulers in Nehemiah 13:11?

What was the response of the people once they saw that the godly leadership had been restored to the Temple?

At this point, what crucial action of commitment did Nehemiah take? (v.14)

Nehemiah's prayer is not a prayer for personal reward, but simply asks God to bless the radical changes he had to make. The cost to Nehemiah was tremendous, but the decision to act was imperative! What instruction are we given in Matthew 16:24, 25 that will assist you in obeying God and not compromising with sin today?

Read Proverbs 3:1-8. Record the verse that speaks to you specifically today. Why?

6. Continue to work on your memory verse for this week. How much can you record without looking?

DAY 6 – BEGIN IN PRAYER

1. Read Nehemiah 13:1-14.

2. What lesson(s) from Nehemiah's life can you apply to your walk this week?

3. The main lesson of chapter 13 is the importance of establishing a daily diligence in our walk with the Lord. How might 2Peter 3:17, 18 serve as a perfect ending to this week's lesson?

What warning is given?

What exhortation needs to be heeded?

4. Record your memory verse and the reference without looking! Can you do it?

DAY 1 – BEGIN IN PRAYER

1. Read Nehemiah 13:15-31.

2. Nehemiah had served as governor and overseer in Jerusalem for 12 years (445-433BC) before being summoned to return to Shushan by King Artaxerxes in the 32nd year of his reign (13:6). Remember the lesson: Daily Diligence Needed! In this second part of chapter 13, what additional spiritual reforms did Nehemiah have to make?

3. What lesson(s) can you learn from this first reading of Nehemiah 13:15-31 that you will be able to apply in your walk with the Lord today?

DAY 2 – BEGIN IN PRAYER

1. Read Nehemiah 13:15-31.

2. According to Nehemiah 13:15-22, what direct command of the LORD were the priests and the people of Jerusalem ignoring?

What do we learn about the covenant of the Sabbath from Exodus 31:13-18?

In Nehemiah's absence, the people had neglected the Temple and their responsibility to support its service. They had also begun to break the Sabbath Law by buying and selling goods on the day that they were commanded to rest and worship the LORD. Review Nehemiah's prayer in Nehemiah 1:5-10, why had the LORD brought judgment on Israel in the first place?

What covenant of repentance had the people made in Nehemiah 10:29-31?

3. According to Nehemiah 13:17, with whom did this reform begin?

The leaders and elders of every church body carry great responsibility for the spiritual direction of the people. What ultimate example are we given of how we ought to serve in John 13:3-17?

Our Lord gave us the perfect example of servant leadership in the life He lived. How is it described?

a. Mark 10:42-45

b. Philippians 2:5-8

c. Ephesians 5:1, 2

4. What is the spiritual criteria for leadership according to 1Timothy 3:1-7?

5. There is nothing wrong with business, it is necessary for life and good stewardship. However, there is a correct time and place for it – it was not to occur on the Sabbath. The people had fallen back to their worldly ways of life. They were no longer leading (by obeying God's commands), they were being led by the unbelieving world around them! What similar distraction might the enemy use today to tempt us to fall away from our commitment to the Lord?

Exodus 20:3 commands us, "You shall have no other gods before Me." What exhortation are you given in 1John 5:21?

What types of things or practices have the potential to become idols or "other gods" in our lives?

Personal: Is there something, someone, or some practice that has taken the number one position in your life? What action do you need to be taking to reorder your priorities?

6. Choose a verse from today's lesson and begin today to commit it to memory!

DAY 3 – BEGIN IN PRAYER

1. Read Nehemiah 13:15-31.

2. In Nehemiah 13:18 Nehemiah declared, did not your fathers do thus, and did not our God bring all this disaster on us and on this city? The people did not learn the lesson from their own history and they now were tempting God to judge their sin in the same manner. What action did Nehemiah take in dealing with the merchants and the sellers in order to protect the people?

Again we see the strong leadership of Nehemiah as he set rules of protection around the people – perhaps, his decisions were very unpopular with the people and most likely with the leaders themselves. Review Hebrews 13:17 – how are we to respond to those leaders the Lord has set over us?

What more do we learn from the following Scriptures regarding the way in which we respond to our leaders in the church?

   a. Hebrews 13:7

   b. 1Thessalonians 5:12, 13

3. Nehemiah's decision was to command that the city gates be closed on the Sabbath. From sundown to sundown no merchants could enter the city. What choice did the merchants make in the first few weeks?

What was Nehemiah's response to their actions?

4. This standoff between Nehemiah and the merchants gives us an excellent illustration of the truth that in the life of every believer sin stands at the door! What warning did the LORD give to Cain regarding the ever present temptation to sin in Genesis 4:6, 7?

Read 1Peter 5:5-11.

What are the exhortations?

What are the warnings?

What are the promises?

5. Nehemiah had to go so far as to threaten those who were trying to tempt the people. What ultimatum did he give? Did it work?

Why do you think it was important that the Levites cleansed themselves (Nehemiah 13:22) in order to go guard the gates?

What further instruction are we given regarding the importance of confession and repentance in the life of a believer?

a. Isaiah 1:16-18

b. Isaiah 55:7-9

c. James 4:8-10

d. 1John 1:9

6. Continue to work on your memory verse for this week. How much can you record without looking?

DAY 4 – BEGIN IN PRAYER

1. Read Nehemiah 13:15-31.

2. As if the breaking of the Sabbath Law was not enough, Nehemiah found even more problems to deal with when he returned from Babylon. The people were intermarrying with those heathen nations around about them. God had clearly forbidden such action. What commitment had they made before the Lord in Nehemiah 10:29, 30?

According to the following Scriptures, why did the LORD demand that His people not marry outside of their faith?

a. Exodus 34:12-16

b. Deuteronomy 7:1-4

3. According to 2Corinthians 6:14-16a, what command is given to the church regarding fellowship and marriage between a believer and an unbeliever?

Why are such relationships forbidden?

What instructions are we given in 2Corinthians 6:16b-18?

4. What strong exhortation is given to us in Ephesians 5:6-11 that will assist us in choosing correct relationships?

5. God's people in Jerusalem had clearly committed to obey His commands, however, time and the influence of the world around them brought them to a place of compromise and sin. According to 1Corinthians 15:33, what is the end result of choosing to keep company with those who do not walk in the ways of the Lord?

As Christians we are to seek our friendships, fellowships, and relationships from those within the church. What is to be our relationship to those who are not yet believers?

a. Matthew 5:16

b. Philippians 2:14, 15

c. 1Peter 2:9-12

6. Continue to work on your memory verse for this week. How much can you record without looking?

DAY 5 - BEGIN IN PRAYER

1. Read Nehemiah 13:15-31.

2. As we finish studying the account of Nehemiah's life, we find him still contending with his stiff-necked people. What severe tactics did he take? (Nehemiah 13:25)

Who did Nehemiah use as a negative example of this terrible sin of the people? (v.26)

3. According to 1Kings 11:1-6, what tragic legacy did King Solomon leave?

King Solomon had every opportunity to obey the Lord, but he did not! Read 1Kings 3:1-15. What could have been the heritage of King Solomon?

Record 1Corinthians 10:12 and use it as a stern reminder that no one is beyond the temptation to fall into sin.

What good news of promise is found in 1Corinthians 10:13?

4. Nehemiah's example shows us that it is important that we learn from the past. It is not necessary that we learn our lessons the hard way! Sadly, too often that is the tragic choice we make! What warning do you find in the following

Scriptures that will keep you from falling into the ways of the world?

a. Proverbs 16:18

b. Proverbs 18:12

c. Proverbs 29:23

How does the example in Peter's life, found in Matthew 26:33-35, remind us that we must always walk in complete dependence upon the Lord and never trust in our own strength?

5. The son of the high priest had married Sanballat's daughter. What action did Nehemiah take against this enemy of Israel?

These were special measures for special times. If you are a believer married to an unbeliever, you have clear instruction to remain, if they are pleased to dwell with you, because your faith will sanctify the other (1Corinthians 7)! However, there are important lessons for us to learn and obey in studying Nehemiah's actions toward this backsliding people of God. What practical steps can you take this week to remove any influence that the world has placed on you or your family?

According to James 5:19, 20, what is your responsibility to others whom the Lord has placed in your life when you see that their lives are becoming entangled with the world?

What was Nehemiah's final prayer according to Nehemiah 13:31?

6. Continue to work on your memory verse for this week. How much can you record without looking?

DAY 6 – BEGIN IN PRAYER

1. Read Nehemiah 13:15-31.

2. What lesson(s) from Nehemiah's life can you apply to your walk this week?

3. The main lesson of chapter 13 is that we are truly convinced of the absolute necessity of a daily spiritual diligence in our walk with the Lord. What does 2Peter 1:5-11 say about this daily diligence?

What promises are given to us in verse 8, 10 & 11?

What warning is found in verse 9?

4. Record your memory verse and the reference without looking! Can you do it?

I pray the Lord has richly blessed you through this study of the Book of Nehemiah!

May you be "Watching and Working" as you continue to faithfully finish the work the Lord has called you to do, and may your response to the enemy's invitations in your life be…

I am doing a great work, so that I cannot come down. Why should the work cease…
Nehemiah 6:3

54774667R00083

Made in the USA
Columbia, SC
05 April 2019